Acknowledgments

Practically everything in this book—stories, photos, documents, data —came from someone who provided it to me, making me profoundly grateful to many, including:

the cousins and others too numerous to list here who responded graciously (even when at first they had no earthly idea who I was), shared their histories, sent materials from their collections, joined in my searches, and became new treasured friends;

the non-profit, governmental, and commercial enterprises that store and make accessible genealogical and archival matter, in particular the Leo Baeck Institute, Yad Vashem, Ancestry.com, National Archives of Australia, the USC Shoah Foundation, Jewish Gen and the Museum of Jewish Heritage, Beit Theresienstadt, and the U.S. Census Bureau;

Frances Keiser of Sagaponack Books & Design whose consummate skills in book production saved me when I had about given up hope of pulling this all together;

my dearest—my husband Howard, son Michael and daughter Rachel —who listened endlessly, usually patiently, to these stories, telling me repeatedly over the years, "You need to write all this down." Now I have.

I am indebted to each person named above and several others for making suggestions and corrections on drafts as this project moved along. It is inevitable, I'm afraid, that inaccuracies remain, but I hope they do not alter the essential truth in these stories. The errors are mine alone.

Finally, this book would not exist without the archive of family photos, letters, documents, and artifacts that my beloved and admired mother, Eleanor Goldberger Friedman, painstakingly organized and lovingly preserved. Above all, she gave me the Tree and she taught me why it matters.

SEARCHING FOR THE MANDLS

June Friedman Entman

Almond Tree
St. Augustine, Florida

Front cover: Photo of Lazar Mandl portrait courtesy of Tony Mandl, Sydney Australia.

Back cover: *The Genealogy of the Family* by Sam Aschkenes, 1952.

ISBNs
979-8-9863585-0-5 (softcover)
979-8-9863585-1-2 (hardcover)
979-8-9863585-2-9 (e-book)

Library of Congress Control Number: 2022918987

Summary: Stories of a Central European Jewish family's migrations, primarily to the U. S. and Australia, from the mid-19th Century to post-WWII. The account describes the immigrants' lives and experiences before and after migration and how the family re-connected in the 21st century.

BIO037000 Biography & Autobiography / Jewish
HIS004000 History / Australia & New Zealand
HIS043000 History / Modern / 20th Century / Holocaust
HIS036040 History / United States / 19th Century
HIS036060 History / United States / 20th Century

Almond Tree
St. Augustine, Florida

Printed in the United States of America
First Edition

To our youngest generation—my grandchildren
Abigail Grace Hatch, Jackson Paul Hatch, and
Alexander George Hatch;

and my first cousins' grandchildren Daniel, Andrew,
and Kristina Catomeris, Morgan Spar, Dylan,
Reece, Andrew, and Travis Goldberger, Anastasia
and Jacob Melnick, Ada and Stella Donnelly,
Vincent, Ethan, and Meridith Goldberger;

and my second cousins' children Joshua and Molly
Lipton, Jason Mandl, Todd Lamberg, Josephine and
Nina Fentriss, Tracy and Megan Mandl:

This book is for you.

As the descendants of Jacob and Henrietta Werner
Mandl, you each are connected to the people and
the stories that follow here. This is a part of your and
your children's heritage, just as all of you are part of
your ancestors' stories.

Suddenly all my ancestors are behind me.
Be still they say. Watch and listen.
You are the result of the love of thousands.

    —Linda Hogan
      Dwellings: A Spiritual History of the Living World

Contents

Preface

As a young girl, I was fascinated by the Mandl-Spitzer Family Tree. I loved seeing my name on a small leaf way at the top surrounded by my brother, cousins, parents, uncles, aunts, and grandparents. I marveled at the long row of large leaves—the great-grandparents. Ten brothers and sisters! The largest family I ever knew had six children, which seemed like an awful lot.

Most of the people on the tree outside of my line—the Jacob Mandl branch—were strangers to me. I wondered who these people were, where they were. Mostly, I pondered the difference in size of the ten branches. Why were some so short with so few leaves compared to the others so tall and thickly leaved?

As I grew older and learned about modern history, I began to understand. Or at least I thought I did. The ten Mandl siblings were born in Central Europe at a time when they, or their children and grandchildren, may have been victims of World War II and Adolf Hitler. We descendants of Jacob Mandl were the lucky ones. Jacob and Henrietta "Yetty" Werner Mandl left Europe to live in America before World War I, when their little girl, my grandmother Nellie, was barely two years old. I surmised that the missing Mandl generations had been lost forever in the Holocaust.

Many years later, when I had retired and had the benefit of time and the family archives my mother had lovingly preserved, plus the Internet with its vast resources, I began to investigate. I had two primary questions:

1. What had happened to the missing Mandls?

2. Why had Jacob Mandl come to America in 1892 while almost none of the other Mandls followed until they had to run for their lives?

This book is the result of that investigation.

I learned that Jacob Mandl came to the U.S. because he married Yetty Werner. Yetty's Werner relatives had, for several generations, been leaving Europe and putting down roots in America. The door was open for Jacob and Yetty to follow. My story then became a tale of two families—the Mandls and the Werners.

Along the way I have uncovered both happy and sad stories, and have made remarkable discoveries. Best of all is that I can report that the lost generations of Mandls were not lost at all; they were merely unknown to me, and largely unknown to each other. Eight of the ten children of Lazar and Therese Spitzer Mandl have living descendants. The Holocaust scattered them around the world, but they are thriving today in North, South, and Central America, Australia, Africa, Europe, and Israel.

If there is a theme to this work, it is one of enduring kindness. There are stories here, on both the Mandl and Werner sides, of people helping relatives, and sometimes mere acquaintances, to escape difficulty and to build new lives in foreign lands. More currently, there are stories of how my search for family has been helped by strangers I have been fortunate to come across.

June Henrietta Friedman Entman
St. Augustine, Florida
2022

Ancestry of Lazar Mandl and Therese Spitzer Mandl

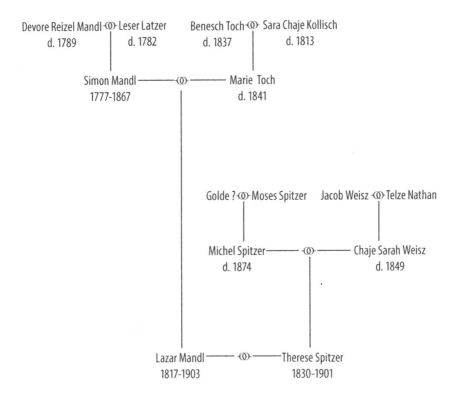

1.

THE TEN MANDLS

Lazar Mandl 1817–1903

Therese Spitzer Mandl 1830–1901

LAZAR AND THERESE SPITZER MANDL raised ten children born between 1850 and 1871—the ten large leaves on the Mandl–Spitzer Family Tree. We know little about Lazar and Therese, only that Lazar was a civil servant—an official of the Jewish community in Senica, a small town in Slovakia, near Vienna,

Austria.[1] We know much more about Lazar and Therese's four daughters and six sons, and their many descendants. By the early 20th century, many of the Mandls were well–educated, prosperous citizens of the Austro–Hungarian Empire.

Jonas Schlafrig 1833–1911   Marie Mandl Schlafrig 1850–1903

The eldest of the ten siblings, **MARIE MANDL**, married Jonas Schlafrig, a physician and leader in the Jewish community in Mistelbach, Austria. Jonas and Marie's six children were talented and accomplished, including a physician, an engineer, and an architect.

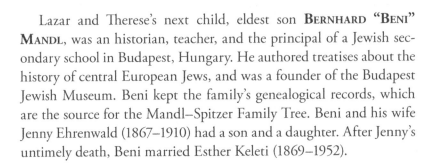

Lazar and Therese's next child, eldest son **BERNHARD "BENI" MANDL**, was an historian, teacher, and the principal of a Jewish secondary school in Budapest, Hungary. He authored treatises about the history of central European Jews, and was a founder of the Budapest Jewish Museum. Beni kept the family's genealogical records, which are the source for the Mandl–Spitzer Family Tree. Beni and his wife Jenny Ehrenwald (1867–1910) had a son and a daughter. After Jenny's untimely death, Beni married Esther Keleti (1869–1952).

Bernhard "Beni" Mandl 1852–1940

Ignatz Aschkenes 1844–1911   Katherina Mandl Aschkenes 1854–1892

KATHERINA MANDL, the third child, married Ignatz Aschkenes, a cantor. Katherina died at age 38, soon after giving birth to their fifth child.

Fourth–born, **AMALIE "MALI"**, is the only one of the ten Mandl siblings whose photograph we do not have. Mali married Max Mandl, most likely a cousin in some degree. Mali and Max had four children; three died young, as did Mali herself in 1900 at age 43. Mali and Max's daughter Hannah Mandl Glasgall, however, escaped the Holocaust along with her husband and two children. Their descendants live today in North and Central America.

HEINRICH MANDL, the fifth child, was the District doctor in Czeszte (Casta), a small town in the Bratislava region of Slovakia. He and his wife Bertha Weisz had five children. Heinrich and his younger brother Simon are the only two of the Mandl siblings with no living descendants; none of their offspring survived the Holocaust.

Heinrich Mandl 1859–1931

Josef Mandl 1861–1923 and Friederike Friedmann Mandl 1870–1934

The sixth–born, **JOSEF MANDL**, and his wife Friederike "Rikki" Friedmann Mandl had a book bindery business in Vienna specializing in gold leaf. Josef and Rikki were parents of two sons and a daughter.

Johanna Mandl 1862–1943

The seventh child, **JOHANNA MANDL**, like her older sister Mali, married a man named Mandl. Johanna and Herman Mandl had two sons and operated a distillery business making slivovitz, a plum brandy, in Uhersky Ostroh, Moravia.

Jacob Mandl 1865–1935   Henrietta "Yetty" Werner Mandl 1867–1939

JACOB MANDL, eighth–born, married Henrietta "Yetty" Werner in 1890 at her family home in Wessely, Moravia, a town 25 miles from Senica where the ten Mandls were born. Jacob and Yetty had six children, including twin boys. Only three of their children–two daughters and one of the twins—lived beyond age two.

Simon Mandl 1867–1924

The ninth sibling, **SIMON MANDL** was a scholar and rabbi in Neutitschein, Moravia. Simon and his wife Rose Baeck had three daughters. Rose was a sister of Rabbi Leo Baeck, renowned leader of Reform Judaism in Germany.[2]

Sermons on the Essence of Judaism 1904 by Simon Mandl dedicated to his parents Lazar and Therese

David Mandl 1871–1945   Clara Schlafrig Mandl 1876–1969

The youngest sibling, **DAVID MANDL**, served in the Austrian army during World War I and later founded a hat manufacturing firm, Sax & Mandl, in Vienna. He was an officer in manufacturing trade associations, and an advisor to Austrian customs authorities. In 1895, David Mandl married Clara Schlafrig, daughter of his oldest sibling, Marie Mandl Schlafrig. While marriage between an uncle and niece would be unusual today, it was not so odd in 19th century Europe. David and Clara had a son and a daughter.

Not all Jewish families in 19th century Austria–Hungary, of course, prospered as did the Mandls. When Lazar and Therese Mandl's son Jacob wed Henrietta "Yetty" Werner in 1890, he married into a family that was not as well off as the Mandls. The Werner family had become part of a surge of Jewish emigration to the United States. Yetty's sister and two brothers, already living in the U.S., were in the third generation of Werners to come to America. Jacob and Yetty soon joined them.

Jacob was the only one of the ten Mandl siblings to leave Europe in the 19th century. Most of the Mandls, well–assimilated and comfortable in Austro–Hungarian society, were not enticed to join the migrations from Europe. Over the next forty years, however, Jacob's decision to become an American was of increasing importance to the Mandls he left behind.

Before continuing with the history of the Mandls, therefore, we turn to the story of the Werner family—how each generation, beginning even before Jacob and Yetty were born, helped younger Werners arriving in the U.S.

Notes

1 Lazar Mandl's father was Reb Simon Mandl (1777–1867). Lazar's son, Bernhard "Beni" Mandl, noted on the family tree he compiled that Simon's father, Reb Leser Latzer of Nikolsburg (Mikulov), Moravia, died in 1782 when Simon, his only child, was 5 years old. Simon then lived in the household of his mother's parents and took their last name–Mandl. Simon's mother, Devore, died when Simon was 12; at 14 he went to study at the Yeshiva in Nikolsburg. Thereafter, Simon became a private tutor in several Moravian towns in and around Hodonin. For a time, he was the private tutor to the Kuffners, a distinguished Jewish family from Lundenberg (Breclav), who were in the distillery, brewery and wool businesses. Simon and his wife Marie Toch had three offspring—son Lazar and daughters Chaje and Chane.

2 After Hitler's rise to power, Leo Baeck refused all offers of escape, declaring that he would stay as long as there was a minyan (quorum of 10 men required for Jewish public worship) of Jews in Germany. In 1933, he was elected founding president of the Representative Council of German Jews. In 1943, Leo Baeck was deported from Berlin to Theresienstadt concentration camp in Czechoslovakia. Although Baeck survived, four of his sisters, including Rose Mandl, died in Theresienstadt.

Werner Family
Immigration to the U.S. 1848-1940

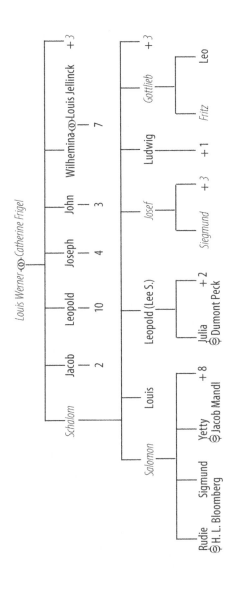

* Names in italics are those who remained in Europe.

2.

COMING TO AMERICA: THREE
GENERATIONS OF WERNERS

Family tree noting Werners in "Amerika," drawn by Siegmund Werner, ca. 1924   1

The Werner family's migration to the United States took place at a time when millions of European Jews were motivated to emigrate. Economic depressions, wars, and political upheavals disrupted the lives of people throughout European society during the 19th century. For Jews in Europe, moreover, antisemitism made things even more difficult. Sometimes there was outright violence, such as "pogroms"—riots incited with the aim of massacring or expelling Jews from a community—especially in Eastern Europe. Often there were legal restrictions on where Jews could live, what trades and professions they could enter, how they could participate in civic society, if at all. Many Jews saw little hope for bettering their lives and for their children's prospects in Europe. Some reacted by seeking a Jewish homeland, giving rise to the Zionist movement to establish such a homeland in Palestine. One of our relatives, Siegmund Werner, was an early leader in that movement. (See Chapter 3.) Others chose to emigrate to countries with more immediate prospects for a better life. The Jewish population of the U.S. ballooned from 15,000 in 1840 to 150,000 in 1860. By 1900, there were 1.5 million Jews living in the U.S.

Emigrating, however, is rarely easy. It is difficult to make one's way in a place where the culture, the social norms, even the language, are all unfamiliar. Some immigrants are trailblazers; they arrive in the new land entirely alone or with few contacts, and yet adapt and succeed. The fortunate immigrant, however, has someone in the new country who encourages him, helps him learn the language, find a place to live, and secure work. Sometimes the help comes from an organization. HIAS, the Hebrew Immigrant Aid Society, was founded in New York in 1881 to assist Jews fleeing religious persecution. Also widespread were "Landsmanshaftn"—associations of people from the same European town or village who joined together to assist new immigrants from the same place. And sometimes, for the lucky ones, there is a family member willing and able to lend a hand.

Stories of the Werner and Mandl families' emigration from Europe include many examples of relatives helping newcomers. For over one hundred years, Werners and Mandls assisted their siblings, nieces and nephews, aunts and uncles, and cousins—some they had never even met—to build new lives in America and elsewhere.

Generation One. In 1848, forty–two years before Yetty Werner and Jacob Mandl were wed in Wessely, Moravia, Yetty's great–uncle Leopold Werner with his wife Lena and two young sons emigrated from Moravia to Utica, a city on upstate New York's Erie Canal. As far as we know, Leopold and Lena were the first in our Werner family to come to the U.S. What sort of assistance, if any, they may have had is unknown. Nevertheless, like others seeking opportunities in the U.S., Leopold gravitated to the Erie Canal corridor. Opened in 1825, the Erie Canal connected the East Coast to the Great Lakes. The canal provided a direct inland water route from New York City to the Midwest, opening up the frontiers of western New York, Ohio, Indiana, Michigan, and points beyond, to immigration and commercial development.

Leopold Werner, like many other Central European Jewish immigrants, was attracted to the garment industry. The surge of Jewish immigration from 1840–60 coincided with invention of the sewing machine and industrialization of the garment industry in the northern United States. Manufacture of clothing, especially menswear, moved from the home to the factory. The need for retail distribution of ready–made goods created opportunities for entrepreneurs. In addition, European Jews were particularly well–suited for the clothing business. Since the late 18th century, Jews had been restricted from many occupations; they were able to make a living primarily by trade in textiles, clothing, and agricultural products such as hides and wool, and in money lending. Jews therefore had expertise in textiles and in business–keeping accounts and selling on credit. These immigrants brought with them the skills needed to meet the rising demand for mass–produced clothing. The manufacturing and retail clothing industry in the United States was primarily Jewish owned by 1870.

After a few years in Utica, Leopold and Lena Werner settled in Buffalo, New York, the western terminus of the Erie Canal on the Great Lakes. They changed the family's name from Werner to Warner, as did all our Werner relatives who later moved to the U.S. In 1854, Leopold Warner founded one of the first clothing manufacturing businesses in Buffalo. When Leopold's brothers John and Joseph later emigrated, they joined him in the business. By 1884, Warner Bros. & Co. had a thousand employees in the manufacture, and wholesale and retail sales of men's clothing. By then, Leopold had retired, and the firm was composed of John Warner and several of Leopold's sons, sons–in–law, and nephews.

Beginning a tradition of civic service in the U.S., Leopold Warner was a charter member and officer of Buffalo's first Reform Jewish congregation, Temple Beth Zion. He was also a founder of the Hebrew

Orphan Asylum of Western New York. When Leopold and Lena celebrated their 50th wedding anniversary in 1892, the lavish affair with ceremony, banquet, and dancing for more than 300 guests was reported in detail in the *Buffalo Express*. The newspaper article noted that in honor of the occasion, the Warners had presented every member of Temple Beth Zion with a handsome Bible and every Sunday–school

Warner Bros. & Co. Building, *Buffalo Morning Express* [NY], Oct. 14, 1888

scholar a book of prayers and hymns, as well as $5,000 donations to the Temple and to the Orphan Asylum. Leopold remained active in Temple Beth Zion until his death in 1900 at age 82.

Temple Beth Zion, Buffalo NY 1890

Generation Two. Back in Moravia, Leopold Werner's brother Schalom was the father of nine.[2] Three of Schalom's sons—Louis, Leopold "Lee S.", and Ludwig—emigrated to America seeking economic opportunity, but not until after their Bar Mitzvahs. Louis, age 18, and Lee, age 13, arrived in the U.S. in 1862, 24 years after their uncle Leopold. Younger brother Ludwig came at age 14 in 1865. Schalom's sons followed their uncle in changing their name from Werner to Warner, and in entering the garment trade in Buffalo, New York.

Louis and Lee S. Werner enroute to America, 1862

Lee S. Warner was particularly successful. After working for others while a teenager in Buffalo, Lee established a retail clothing store in Effingham, Illinois. Lee was joined in Effingham by his brothers Louis and Ludwig. The Effingham, Illinois census of 1870 lists Louis, age 26, and Leopold, age 22, as dealers in clothing and Ludwig Warner, age 18, as a store clerk.[3] Lee and Ludwig were also partners with other Warners in the manufacturing business in Buffalo. In Crawfordsville, Indiana, where he began yet another clothing business in 1893, Lee partnered with Dumont Peck, his daughter Julia's husband.[4] Lee was a devoted Mason and member of several other fraternal orders. When he died at his home in Crawfordsville in 1921, the local newspaper recounted both Lee's commercial successes and civic activities.

LEOPOLD S. WARNER LEADING BUSINESS MAN PASSES AWAY

SENIOR MEMBER OF FIRM OF WARNER & PECK VICTIM OF HEART TROUBLE AND PNEUMONIA.

ACTIVE MEMBER OF MASONS AND OTHER ORGANIZATIONS

Funeral Services Will be Held at Temple at 3 O'clock Friday—Interment at Buffalo.

Lee S. Warner, senior member of the firm of Warner & Peck, clothiers, died at his home, 706 east Main street, at 6:20 o'clock this morning after suffering an illness of two weeks' duration from heart disease which was complicated towards the last by an attack of pneumonia.

He was one of the best known business men in the city and was the founder of the clothing firm which bears his name and that of his son-in-law, Dumont M. Peck.

A Masonic service will be conducted at the Temple Friday afternoon at 3 o'clock to which the public is invited. The body will lie in state at the temple from 1 o'clock. After the services the remains will be taken by the family to Buffalo, N. Y., where burial will be made at Forest Lawn cemetery.

Leopold S. Warner was born in Austria, near Vienna, July 26, 1849. He came to this country at the age of 13 years, lived in New York for a time, then went to Savannah, Ga., and later to Buffalo, N. Y. He became a naturalized citizen at the age of 21 years and at 24 years of age was operating a clothing store at Effingham, Ill., under the name of L. Warner & Bro. At the age of 30 he returned to Buffalo and entered the manufacturing business in the firm of Warner, Sellinek & Warner, manufacturers of trousers. In January, 1893, he came to Crawfordsville and purchased the clothing store of Joly Joel. He conducted the business until 1900 when he formed a partnership with his son-in-law, Dumont M. Peck under the name of Warner & Peck. He was active in the business of the firm until his death.

He was married to Rachael Wiener of Buffalo on August 21, 1873, who with three children, Mrs. Juliet Warner Peck of Crawfordsville, Mrs. William Brinkley of Indianapolis and Sidney M. Warner of Akron, Ohio, survive him. He has one grandson, David Warner Peck, of Crawfordsville.

He was a Mason for over fifty years and a most devoted member of the order. He belonged to Washington Lodge No. 240 of Buffalo until he became a member of Montgomery Lodge No. 50. He was also a member of the council. He also held membership in the Odd Fellows, Elks, Ben-Hur, Court of Honor and Forty-Niners.

Lee Warner obituary, *Crawfordsville Daily Journal* [IN], Nov. 3, 1921

Buffalo Evening News [NY], May 5, 1890

Lee Warner also stayed in touch with his family in Europe, returning at least once for a visit with family in 1906.[5] Lee's nephew Siegmund Werner (son of Lee's brother Josef) noted in a 1924 memoir that "Leopold [Lee] was really well off. He visited us once in Europe and met some of the family. He ... kept regular correspondence with my Father until near his [Lee's] death in 1922 in USA."[6] Interviewed by the *Crawfordsville (Indiana) Journal* in August 1914 at the outbreak of World War I, Lee expressed great concern for his brother Gottlieb in Vienna, both for Gottlieb's banking business and for Gottlieb's two sons in the Austrian military. He was quoted, "During the past few days I have been worrying a great deal about my brother and his family. I have not heard from them for more than two weeks now . . . I wish they were all safe out of the country."[7]

Lee S. Warner and grandson David Peck ca. 1905   Ludwig Werner

Generation Three. Family history repeated when Lee and Ludwig Warner helped their brother Salomon's children become Americans, just as their uncle Leopold had helped them. In September 1878, Salomon Werner brought his two oldest children, Rudolphine "Rudie", age 14, and Siegmund "Sig",[8] age 13, to America from their home in Wessely, Moravia.

S.S. City of Brussels, the ship that brought Salomon, Rudie and Sig Werner to America in 1878

Salomon returned home to his wife Betty and six younger children in Wessely, while Rudie and Sig became members of their uncles' households. The 1880 U.S. Census for Buffalo, New York shows Rudie living with Lee and his wife and young children, and Sig living with Ludwig and his family. Both households also included a live–in servant.

Rudie Warner ca. 1884   Sig Warner ca. 1890

Rudie Warner married Henry A. Bloomberg, an immigrant from Hungary, in Buffalo in 1888. Rudie and Henry went to live in Orrville, Ohio where Henry and his brothers, like the Warners, were in the retail dry goods business. Sig Warner also moved west. After working in Warner family businesses in New York and Indiana, Sig relocated to the Oklahoma Territory where he himself became a retail business entrepreneur. By 1895, Sig Warner and Rudie Bloomberg were joined in the U.S. by their five younger sisters and their widowed mother Betty.

Notes

1 Original in Siegmund Werner, *Familientafel*, 1924, Leo Baeck Institute, Memoir Collection, ME954, Center for Jewish History NYC.

2 Schalom Werner, originally from Bisenz, was the Toll Collector on the River March in Wessely (Veseli nad Moravou). His wife Sibbel Geiduschek (also known as Julie Gedusche) was understood by her grandson Siegmund Werner to have been the "Queen" and ruler of the family—distinguished, good–looking, reader of French and German literature. Both died young, Julie at 53 and Schalom during an operation at the Fuerth Sanatorium, before Siegmund was born in 1867.

3 Louis died at age 35 in 1880; his gravestone in Buffalo's Forest Lawn Cemetery reads, "Our Brother Lewis Warner."

4 Dumont and Julia's only child, David Warner Peck, graduated from Harvard Law School in 1925, was a partner at age 31 in the NY law firm Sullivan and Cromwell, and served as Presiding Justice of the Appellate Division of the NY Supreme Court.

5 Lee S. Warner, age 50, was issued a U.S. passport in June 1906 and appears on the passenger list of the *Kaiser Wilhelm* sailing from Bremen Germany to New York Sept. 4–11, 1906.

6 Siegmund Werner, *Familientafel*, 1924, Leo Baeck Institute, Memoir Collection, ME954, Center for Jewish History NYC.

7 Gottlieb's son Fritz died after a short illness in 1917 and Gottlieb died in 1918. Gottlieb's son Leo Werner, a watchmaker, came to the U.S. via Shanghai in 1940 along with his wife and two teenage children.

8 Brothers Salomon and Josef Werner both had sons named Siegmund (or Sigmund), born in 1867 and 1865 respectively.

Werner Cousins in Chapter 3

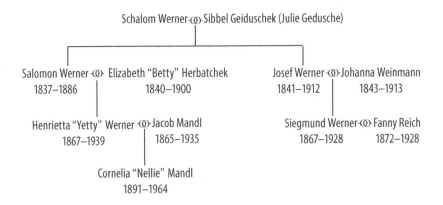

Schalom Werner ∞ Sibbel Geiduschek (Julie Gedusche)

Salomon Werner ∞ Elizabeth "Betty" Herbatchek
1837–1886   1840–1900

Josef Werner ∞ Johanna Weinmann
1841–1912   1843–1913

Henrietta "Yetty" Werner ∞ Jacob Mandl
1867–1939   1865–1935

Siegmund Werner ∞ Fanny Reich
1867–1928   1872–1928

Cornelia "Nellie" Mandl
1891–1964

3.

AN DER WIEGE: SIEGMUND WERNER CELEBRATES THE BIRTH OF NELLIE MANDL

After Salomon Werner returned from taking Rudie and Sig to America in 1878, six children remained with him and Betty Werner in Wessely.[1]

Salomon and Betty Werner with, in age order,
Yetty, Wilhelm, Hannah, Pauline, Eda and Katherine, ca.1882

Salomon Werner died in 1886 at age 49. Yetty, Betty's oldest child still at home, married Jacob Mandl in 1890 and gave birth to Cornelia "Nellie" Mandl in Wessely on February 20, 1891. In honor of the occasion, Siegmund Werner, one of the many Werner cousins,[2] wrote a poem for the new parents entitled *An der Wiege (At the Cradle)* celebrating the renewal of life. When he wrote *An der Wiege,* 24–year–old Siegmund Werner was a student at the University of Vienna, but he had a special connection to his cousins in Wessely.

An der Wiege (At the Cradle)

Siegmund Werner and fiancée Fanny Reich, 1893

In 1874, when Siegmund was seven years old, his parents' grain business in Vienna failed. They were forced to sell both home and business and start over. While Siegmund's parents moved their household and opened a new business in Baden, they sent Siegmund to live with his Uncle Salomon and Aunt Betty Werner in the small town of Wessely. Salomon brought young Siegmund from Vienna to Wessely by railway and horse cart. Siegmund stayed in Wessely for less than a year, rejoining his parents and siblings after they were settled in Baden.

Elizabeth "Betty" Herbatchek Werner   Siegmund Werner, 1874

In 1924, at age 57, Siegmund authored a memoir that included a discussion of his childhood sojourn in Wessely.[3] He wrote about missing his family and being unhappy in his new school. He also recalled how Uncle Salomon helped him with his academic shortcomings, especially in Hebrew and handwriting, and the kindness of his Aunt Betty. He became particularly fond of his oldest cousin Rudie, who demonstrated a "soft and motherly attitude" towards him. Of her, he wrote, "One gesture, one word made me forget my sorrows or troubles." Although Siegmund's stay in Wessely was not long, he remained close to his cousins from Wessely, rejoicing in the birth of Yetty's daughter seventeen years later. Siegmund also recalled, even 50 years later, his deep affection for cousin Rudie, who had emigrated to America not long after Siegmund's time in Wessely.

Siegmund Werner completed his studies in medicine in 1896. While a student, he joined the Zionist movement seeking establishment of a Jewish state in Palestine. Siegmund became a close associate of Theodore Herzl, founder of the World Zionist Organization, who is considered the father of the State of Israel. Siegmund participated in the World Zionist Congress in Basel Switzerland and was Editor of Herzl's newspaper *Die Welt* (*The World*). He was at Herzl's side at his death in 1904.

Siegmund Werner and Theodore Herzl

Siegmund Werner–Theodore Herzl Correspondence

Later, Siegmund moved to Iglau, Moravia (now Jihlava, Czech Republic), where he practiced dentistry while continuing his Zionist activities.[4] During World War I, Siegmund served as a medical officer in the Austrian army. He continued to write poetry throughout his life, including a 1903 book entitled "Ruth, und andere Gedichte" (Ruth, and Other Poems).

Siegmund Werner's medical practice in Iglau, Moravia

Siegmund and Fanny Werner had three children—Edith, Theodore (named for Herzl), and Robert. Before any of Siegmund's children were born, however, all of his Wessely cousins—including the child whose birth inspired *An der Wiege*—had left for America, and the families eventually lost touch. Siegmund died in Iglau in 1928. Siegmund's handwritten poem celebrating Nellie Mandl's birth in Wessely in 1891 was kept by the family in America. Nellie's American granddaughter was able to share the poem with Siegmund's British grandson when, as described in the next chapter, they discovered each other more than a century after Nellie's birth.

At the Cradle[5]

Full of thought, I stand at this cradle,
which will soon be rocking with a dear child
and I am gripped by the most beautiful of all victories
for which nature controls herself and wrestles.

That is her cycle, that is her well-planned goal,
that nothing can ever decay, in spite of death and ending,
and so truth is the eternal life
which the human spirit invented to console itself.

We are immortal! What great hope!
Because new buds always burst into blossom.
Even if a branch dies, a thousand blossoms are already open
in its place in a multitude of color.

And you who shall dream here, sweet blossom,
until the sun of understanding kisses you into maturity
Oh, may a happy fate protect you
and mete pain out to you only sparingly.

Then someday you will stand at a cradle,
as I stand here today, silently amazed and moved
and you will see with clear eyes
how end and beginning touch each other.

Feb. 23, 1891

SW

Notes

1 The 1900 U.S. Census indicates that Betty Werner (then Warner) gave birth to 11 children, of whom 8 were then living. Of her daughter Yetty Mandl's 6 children, 3 did not live to age 2. See Chapter 6.

2 Yetty Werner Mandl had both a brother and a cousin named Siegmund Werner. Yetty's brother Siegmund, born in 1865, was living in America when Yetty's daughter Nellie was born in Wessely. Yetty's cousin Siegmund was the son of Salomon's brother Josef Werner.

3 Siegmund Werner's handwritten memoir in German, *Familientafel*, 1924, is located at the Leo Baeck Institute, Memoir Collection, ME 954, Center for Jewish History, NYC.

4 Hugo Gold (ed.), *Die Juden und Judengemeinden Maehrens* (1929), 249–50.

5 English translation by Charles Winter, a Mandl cousin discussed in Chapter 10.

Werner Cousins in Chapter 4

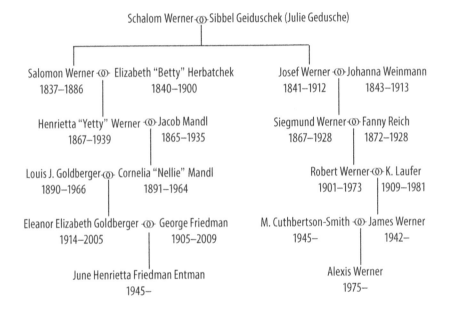

4.

FINDING SALOMON WERNER'S GRAVESTONE:
A STORY OF DISCOVERY
AND A KINDNESS RETURNED

This chapter and the next are stories about how 5th generation Werner descendants, previously unknown to each other, established contact in the 21st century and filled in missing pieces of the family's history. This first story begins with a photograph of Salomon Werner's 1886 gravestone in the Wessely, Moravia cemetery.

Salomon Werner gravestone ca. 1887
Jewish Cemetery, Veseli nad
Moravou (Wessely), CZ

In 1895, when Betty Werner left Wessely with her two youngest daughters to join her six children living in America, she brought along photographs of her husband Salomon and of his gravestone.[1] By 2006, I had inherited these two photos, along with other Werner photos and artifacts.

Salomon Werner 1837–1886

Knowing that my grandmother Nellie was born in Wessely, Moravia to Jacob and Henrietta Werner Mandl, I set out to find Werner connections. I began with the Jewish Gen website (https://www.jewishgen.org/), on which one can post surnames and places, and contact others with the same research interests. The website led me to a researcher who had listed the surname Werner and the place Wessely. He turned out to be my cousin James Werner, born in Great Britain in 1942, three years before me.

James and I quickly discovered that we had copies of some of the same 19th Century photographs. We were descended from brothers—his great–grandfather Josef Werner and my great–great grandfather Salomon Werner. It was incredibly exciting when several of my previously–unidentifed photos popped up on the computer screen attached to an email from my newly–discovered cousin across the Atlantic. James' copies were fortunately better identified than mine.

James' grandfather was Siegmund Werner, who in 1891 penned the poem celebrating my grandmother Nellie's birth in Wessely. Siegmund's son Robert emigrated in 1934 from Vienna to Britain where he married, served in the Royal Air Force during WWII, and raised his three children, David, Jane, and James. James grew up knowing little about his Jewish heritage. When he began to research his roots in the late 1990's, James learned that his grandfather Siegmund had been a journalist, poet, physician, and a distinguished leader of the Zionist movement.

In 2004, James discovered a collection of the papers of Eric Werner, Siegmund Werner's nephew, in New York.[2] Eric Werner, born in Vienna in 1901, was a noted composer and authority on sacred music when he emigrated to the U.S. in 1938.[3] Among Eric Werner's papers, James Werner discovered Siegmund Werner's memoir handwritten in 1924, four years before Siegmund's death at age 60.[4]

Siegmund Werner's memoir is an invaluable resource for Werner family history. It contains detailed family trees and descriptions of the extended family. The memoir discusses daily life and public events in Wessely, Baden, and Vienna, and gives insights into political, social, and economic upheavals, including the antisemitic climate of those times.

In the Spring of 2006, James came for a visit to my home in Tennessee. He brought copies of Siegmund Werner's memoir, and English translations of the first 50 or so pages, about one–third of the manuscript. The translated portion includes the story of Siegmund's sojourn as a child with his Uncle Salomon and Aunt Betty Werner in Wessely, and reveals how even fifty years later, he felt the kindness of his Wessely relatives.

In 2011, James wrote to me that he and his son Alexis would soon be traveling to Central Europe to visit several sites connected with the family, including Iglau (now Jihlava, Czech Republic), where Siegmund practiced dentistry and James' father was born. Shortly thereafter, I realized that they might travel not far from Wessely (now Veseli nad Moravou, Czech Republic). I emailed James, attaching the photo of Salomon's gravestone and asked if they might stop to see if it was still there. James replied,

We are here in Budapest, and are leaving for Jihlava in the morning!!! Will try to swing by en route!! You are just in time. :) Will get back to you.

That night, James emailed:

We arrived at Wessely in 30+ [Celsius, 86 F] degrees. Very hot indeed … no one spoke any language apart from Czech. We eventually managed to link up with the Gate Keeper who let us into the cemetery. A well guarded and maintained site. No sign of the grave. No name or photo recognition from the keeper. We were just about to give up when Alexis who was standing on a pile of stones spotted the next grave shown in your photo. He realized that he might be standing on it and started to clear the undergrowth. Lo and behold!! The very same stone, tumbled down and covered. So here you have it. I have arranged with the man to re–erect the stone. He assures me, if I understood correctly, that it will be done!!!

Alexis Werner & Dr. Vilem Reichsfeld, Jewish Cemetery, Veseli nad Moravou, CZ, June 2011

Dr. Vilem Reichsfeld, of the Veseli nad Moravou city council, kept his promise. In July, 2011, he sent photos of Salomon Werner's restored gravestone.

Salomon Werner gravestone, Veseli 2011

The Hebrew text on Salomon's gravestone reads in English:

Here lies an honest and righteous man, a God fearing friend. Reb Zalmen Werner died with a good name, to the endless sorrow of his wife and children, on the 28th day of Nisan 5646. Beneath this marker lies a treasured soul. Our father, our guide, left us in but half his days. Though God's hand touched him with suffering, he never complained. All his life on Earth he walked in the ways of righteousness, his heart one with his Creator and his people. His soul shall live forever.

One hundred thirty years after Uncle Salomon and Aunt Betty cared for a young Siegmund Werner in their home in Wessely, Siegmund's grandson and great–grandson, James and Alexis, returned the kindness. Twenty–first century Werners honored their nineteenth century relative by rescuing his monument from where it lay, buried under rubble but intact, in the Wessely Jewish cemetery.[5]

Veseli nad Moravou (Wessely), CZ

Notes

1 In her 1941 Last Will, Eda Werner Perilstein of Orrville, Ohio, who was 10 years old when her father Salomon Werner died, left a $200 endowment to the Cemetery Association of Wessely for her father's grave.

2 Eric Werner Collection, AR 2179, MF 523, Leo Baeck Institute, Center for Jewish History.

3 Eric Werner founded the School of Sacred Music of Hebrew Union College, and set up the musicology department at Tel Aviv University in Israel.

4 Siegmund's memoir, *Familientafel*, 1924, has since been relocated from the Eric Werner Collection to the LBI's Memoir Collection, ME 954, Leo Baeck Institute, Center for Jewish History, NYC.

5 In a notation on his family tree reproduced at the beginning of Chapter 2 in this book, Siegmund Werner wrote [English translation]: "On September 2, 1924, I visited the graves of my grandparents [Schalom and Sibbel Werner] in the cemetery in Veseli nad Moravou. They were sunken and levelled because they were overgrown with grass so that the bases of the small gravestones were completely in the ground." In 2022, Vilem Reichsfeld confirmed that Schalom's and Sibbel's gravestones could not be located. Dr. Reichsfeld explained that the "small tombstones in the cemetery are made of sandstone, which is very much influenced by nature and many of them are irretrievably destroyed or illegible."

Werner Cousins in Chapter 5

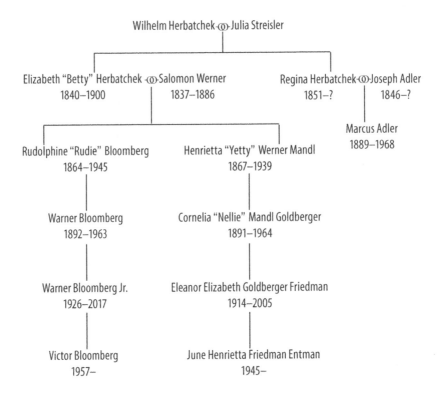

5.

RUDIE WERNER BLOOMBERG'S PHOTO ALBUM:
ANOTHER DISCOVERY, ANOTHER KINDNESS

This is another genealogy success story, perhaps even more remarkable than finding Salomon Werner's gravestone intact under the rubble in Veseli nad Moravou.

I began to search for Werner relatives in the U.S. in 2006. Because my great–grandmother Yetty Werner Mandl had seven siblings who also emigrated to America, I thought there was a good chance of finding Werner cousins in this country. At first, all I had to go on were:

1. that Jacob and Yetty Werner Mandl lived for several years in Orrville, Ohio before moving to New York City,
2. a few 1950s–era letters between my grandmother Nellie Mandl Goldberger in New York and some of her aunts and cousins in Ohio and California, and
3. an entry in Nellie's 1950 address book for a Warner Bloomberg in Massillon, Ohio.

Research revealed that Yetty's sister Rudie and her husband Henry Bloomberg raised four children in Ohio–a son, Warner Solomon Bloomberg, and daughters Adeline, Marguerite, and Isabel. Of the four, only Warner had children. By 1935, Henry and Rudie had retired and were living with Adeline in Los Angeles, California.

Warner and Isabel remained in the Midwest. Henry and Rudie died in Los Angeles in 1940 and 1945 respectively. Adeline and Marguerite also died in Los Angeles, in 1974 and 1976.

On the internet, I found a Warner S. Bloomberg Jr., a retired professor of sociology, in San Diego, and a Warner S. Bloomberg III, an attorney, in San Jose, California. I mailed letters to each of them at the addresses available online, but I received no responses. At that point, I abandoned the search for Rudie's descendants.

Sometime around 2010, I uploaded the Mandl–Werner family tree to Ancestry.com, where other interested family members could see it and connect with people researching the same individuals. On May 25, 2012, I received the following message from a complete stranger via Ancestry.com:

Are you descended from Rudolphine Werner Bloomberg? I have family pictures from an album retrieved from a trash can in Los Angeles about 40 years ago and I would like to return it to someone descended from her.

I replied that Rudolphine was my great–grandmother's sister, that I knew of no living descendants of hers, and I would love to have the album. My correspondent, Anne Ginchereau, replied:

Dear June,

[…]

I can't wait for you to see the album … you will see when it arrives that it is something special. It contains photos dating back to the mid 1800's from Austria and Czechoslovakia (I think), and later pictures from New York, Ohio, Oklahoma and other places. […] There is a handwritten chart showing descendants of Solomon Warner's father and his siblings.

The history of the album in our family is that Lucie Morris (a family friend) saw it sticking out of a trash can sometime in the 1970's, I think. She was interested in genealogy and couldn't bear to think of it being destroyed so she retrieved it. When Lucie died in 1992, my great–aunt was executor of her estate and she took the album and held on to it.

My mother came across it while helping my great–aunt and uncle clean out their garage and decided it was time to try to find someone related to the family, so she copied a few pages and sent them to me.

Anyway, I am so happy to be able to restore it to a good owner […]

I suppose that either Adeline or Marguerite inherited the album when their parents died in the 1940's. As neither of the sisters had husbands or children when they died in the 1970's, the album apparently became the victim of an estate disposal.

Rudie's album: Four photos of Rudie's mother, Betty Herbatchek Werner, with one in upper left of Betty's mother, Julia Streisler Herbatchek, and one in lower left of Betty's husband, Salomon Werner.

Rudie's album has 38 pages like the one pictured on the preceding page with photos dating from the 1860's to the 1930's. Rudie captioned most of the photographs, although some of the captions are lost to the crumbling edges of the pages. Rudie's hand drawn family trees are mostly intact.

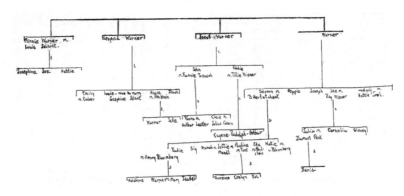

Rudie Bloomberg's Werner and Herbatchek family trees

In 2017, five years after Rudie's album traveled from California to me in Florida, I received a message out of the blue from Warner Bloomberg Jr.'s son Victor. Victor had just found my 2006 letter in his 91–year–old father's desk–eleven years after I sent the letter! Victor Bloomberg, my new–found third cousin, and I met electronically and shared family histories. I was more than happy to return Rudie's album to her grandson and great–grandsons in California before Warner Jr. passed away the following year.

Rudie's album is a treasure. Many of the photos in this book come from that album. I already had copies of several of the album photos, but I had no idea who was depicted in some of them. Because of Rudie (and the strangers who rescued her album), I now know whose portraits I have and how I am related to them. Thanks to Rudie, we have photos of a direct female line for eight generations. It began with a mid–19th century photo of my great–great–great grandmother, Julia Streisler (Mrs. Wilhelm Herbatchek):

Julia Streisler
(Mrs. Wilhelm Herbatchek)

Julia's daughter
Elizabeth "Betty" Herbatchek, ca. 1870
(Mrs. Salomon Werner)

Betty's daughter,
Henrietta "Yetty" Werner, ca. 1886
(Mrs. Jacob Mandl)

Yetty's daughter,
Cornelia "Nellie" Mandl, 1912
(Mrs. Louis J. Goldberger)

Nellie's daughter
Eleanor Elizabeth Goldberger, 1932,
(Mrs. George Friedman)

Eleanor's daughter
June Henrietta Friedman, 1966
(Mrs. Howard Entman)

June's daughter
Rachel Entman, 1993
(Mrs. Ryan Hatch)

Rachel's daughter
Abigail Grace Hatch, 2021

Rudie's album also introduced me to my Herbatchek relations and solved one of my photo identifying mysteries. Writing on the photo below identifies the children as my grandmother Nellie Mandl (Goldberger) and Mark Adler. I had no idea who Mark Adler might be.

I learned from Rudie's family trees that Nellie's grandmother Betty Herbatchek Werner had a sister Regina. After coming to the U.S. in 1863, Regina married Joseph David Adler. The Adlers lived in New York City with their eight children. Marcus Hirsh Adler was Nellie's cousin, the youngest son of Joseph and Regina Herbatchek Adler.

Cousins
Mark Adler and Nellie Mandl, ca. 1895

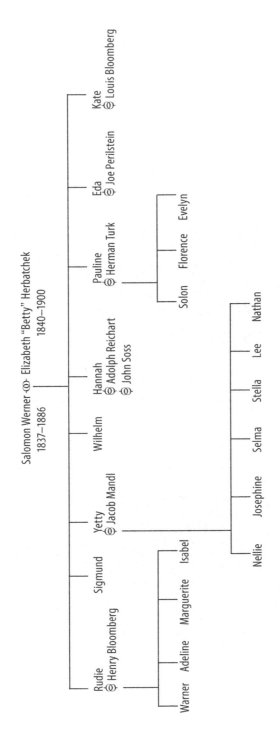

6.

THE WERNERS IN EARLY 20TH CENTURY AMERICA

By May of 1895, Rudie Warner Bloomberg's widowed mother and all of Rudie's siblings had arrived in America. Like Rudie's Warner uncles who operated retail clothing stores in a number of cities, her husband Henry Bloomberg and his three brothers founded clothing stores in several Ohio cities. Henry and Rudie raised their family of four in Orrville and nearby Massillon, Ohio where they were active in civic and Jewish community and charitable organizations.

Rudie and Henry Bloomberg, standing center, with their children Adeline,
Marguerite, Isabel, and Warner Bloomberg, Massillon, Ohio, ca. 1919

Rudie's brother Siegmund, who had arrived with her in 1878, moved on from Buffalo, New York to Crawfordsville, Indiana, and then to the Oklahoma Territory, where he went into the dry goods business with Herman Turk, a Hungarian immigrant. In 1905, when the federal government was selling public lands to private parties prior to Oklahoma's statehood, Sig Warner purchased a 160–acre plot in Greer County in far western Oklahoma. After Sig died in 1928, the farm was sold and the proceeds distributed to his sisters.

Pauline Werner arrived in 1891, and married Sig's partner, Herman Turk, in 1892. They settled in Oklahoma, where Herman owned several businesses in partnership with Turk relatives. One business was Little Sam's Saloon in Lexington, Oklahoma, and another a grocery store just across the river in Purcell. When he purchased the grocery in 1914, the local paper described Herman as "an old timer in this country … well acquainted with the people on both sides of the river and we predict a successful outcome of his business career."[1]

Herman and Pauline Werner Turk with Solon, Florence, and Evelyn, Tulsa, Oklahoma, ca. 1903

The last to emigrate was the Werners' widowed mother Elizabeth "Betty" who arrived in Ohio in May 1895 along with her two youngest children, Eda and Katie, ages 20 and 18.[2] Eda married Joe Perilstein in 1899. They lived in Orrville where Joe was in the dry goods business, at times partnered with the Bloombergs. Katie married Louis Bloomberg, Henry's youngest brother and business partner, in 1900.

Joe and Eda Werner Perilstein, ca. 1900

Bloomberg ad in *The Evening Repository*, [Canton, OH], Oct. 14, 1904

Louis and Kate Werner Bloomberg, ca. 1930

Yetty Werner's husband Jacob Mandl came to Orrville in 1892 and went to work in Henry Bloomberg's clothing store. Yetty and their two young daughters—Cornelia "Nellie" and Selma—joined Jacob in Orrville in March 1893. Despite the Warner family's apparent success, Jacob and Yetty Mandl's early years in the U.S. were not easy. Not long after Yetty and the children arrived in Orrville, they traveled to Oklahoma City, in the Oklahoma Territory, where Yetty's brother Sig Warner and sister Pauline Turk were living. While there, on April 5, 1893, one–year old Selma died.

Jacob and Yetty sent this photo of 2–year–old Nellie back to Wessely with a note on the back, "A lot of kisses to grandma and auntis Eda and Kate from Nelly, Oklahoma City, O.T., July 7, 1893."

Nellie Mandl, 1893

On January 24, 1894 in New York City, Yetty gave birth to another daughter, Josephine, who died in March 1895 of whooping cough. Daughter Stella was born in New York in August 1895 and the family returned to Orrville, where they lived until 1899. In October 1897, Yetty had twin boys–Salomon Nathan and Simon Lee Mandl; Salomon Nathan died of cholera at 11 months.

Standing: Nellie and Stella Mandl, with brothers Lee and Nathan, Orville, Ohio, 1898

ORRVILLE PUBLIC SCHOOLS.

Monthly Report of

Nellie Mandel

Beginning _Sept. 5,_ Ending _May 31._

	1	2	3	4	5	6	7	8	9
Half Days Present	38	40	40	40	40	31	40	40	40
Times Tardy	0	0	0	0	0	0	0	0	1
Deportment	98	97	98	99	96	97	98	98	96
Punctuality	100	100	100	100	100	100	100	100	98
Spelling	96	94	96	96	90	98	94	92	86
Reading	94	94	96	95	96	94	96	95	95
Writing	92	92	93	94	92	93	94	94	94
Language	92	93	92	96	93	94	95	94	90
Arithmetic	92	93	92	94	90	93	88	92	90
Geography	_Retoricals_			94	96	94			95

Nellie Mandl 3rd grade, 1898–99

By 1900, Jacob and Yetty had returned to New York City, where they raised their three surviving children and lived for the rest of their lives. Whether they preferred the big city, or Jacob was not suited to the family mercantile business, or there was some other reason to leave Ohio, we do not know.[3] Jacob's first employment in New York was as a street car conductor. By 1905, he worked as a postal carrier and later for many years in the post office.

Jacob and Yetty Werner Mandl,
with their children
Nellie, Stella, and Lee,
New York NY, ca. 1905

Yetty and Jacob Mandl
with their first grandchild
Herbert Goldberger, 1914

Living in New York City allowed the Mandls to become involved in the larger Jewish community there. Jacob, originally from Szenice,[4] Slovakia, was a founder and President of the Szeniczer Sick and Benevolent Association. The Association was one of the many organizations, known as "landsmanshaft," formed by people from the same town in Europe. The organizations' purposes were both social and charitable, providing financial and emotional support to their immigrant members, and burial benefits in cemetery plots purchased and maintained by the society. "J. Mandl, Pres." is carved on the portal of the Szeniczer Sick and Benevolent Association section of Mt. Hebron Cemetery in Queens, New York.

Szeniczer Society portal, Mt. Hebron Cemetery Queens NY

Jacob Mandl (arrow), Szeniczer Sick and Benevolent Society, 1920s

The Warner sisters—Yetty and Hannah in New York; Rudie, Pauline, Eda, and Katie in the West—stayed in touch throughout their lives. The *Orrville Courier* newspaper of October 13, 1922 reported, "Mrs. Jacob Mandle [Yetty Mandl] of New York left Wednesday for Massillon [Ohio] after spending the past week with her sister Mrs. Joseph Perilstein [Eda]. She will visit another sister, Mrs. H.A. Bloomberg [Rudie] at Massillon before returning home."

Yetty's daughter Nellie maintained a lively and affectionate correspondence with her western aunts and cousins—Rudie's daughters Adeline, Marguerite and Isabel in Ohio and California, and Pauline's daughters Florence and Evelyn in Oklahoma. When Nellie's daughter Eleanor Goldberger was engaged to be married in 1940, Eda wrote to her niece Nellie,

To tell you that we are exceedingly happy would be putting it mildly over the happy news of dear Eleanors engagement. We are more sorry now than ever that we did not meet your dear daughter last summer, but judging by her aunt Kate's description, she must be nigh perfection and a lovely girl—and accordingly she will be happy–for girls of her type generally attract men of similar character. So may God shower blessings of all good things upon the pair, so they be a source of happiness to their dear unselfish parents also. Kate [said] she just could shout and cry with joy because she loves Eleanor, that she is the finest girl she ever knew, and Eleanors happiness is her very own also. That coming from your aunt Kate has a great significance.

Wedding of Eleanor Elizabeth Goldberger and George Friedman, New York, NY, 1940

Notes

1 The *Purcell Register* [OK], Dec. 10, 1914. Solon, namesake of an archaic Athenian statesman and lawmaker, fittingly graduated with a law degree and high honors from the University of Oklahoma in 1914. Twenty–five year-old Solon served in France as a sergeant in the U.S. Army during WWI. He returned home in 1918 to practice law in Purcell and Oklahoma City until his untimely death at age 43 in 1933. *Lexington Leader* [OK], June 15, 1915; *Daily Transcript* [Norman, OK], July 13, 1918; *Purcell Register* [OK], Aug. 29, 1918. Solon's sisters, Florence and Evelyn, graduated from Lexington High School, married, and operated mercantile businesses in Oklahoma. Of the three, only Evelyn had offspring, a son Mervin Friedman

2 Two others of Salomon and Betty's children arrived earlier. The family lost contact with Wilhelm shortly after he came to the U.S. Hannah arrived in 1886 and lived in New York City until her death in 1944. She married Adolph Reichardt, a baker, in 1895 and after he died in 1913, married John Soss.

3 When Nellie Mandl Goldberger moved from New York to Atlanta, Georgia in 1962, her first cousin Florence Turk Simons wrote to her: "I never thought that anything could move you out of New York. Mother [Pauline Werner Turk] used to tell me how she tried to persuade your folks [Jacob and Yetty Werner Mandl] to come West but your dear mother said she would rather be in New York than any place in the world."

4 Szenice is the Hungarian–language name of the town, also called Senica in Slovak, and Senitz in German.

The Mandls in Chapter 7

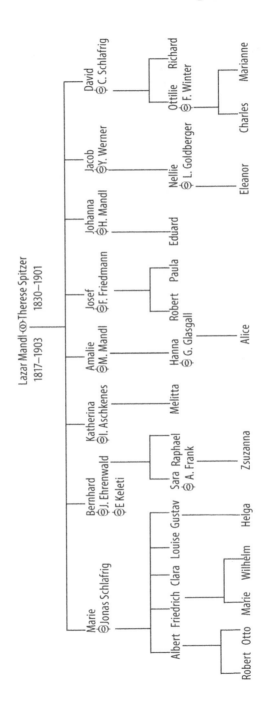

7.

THE MANDLS IN EARLY 20TH CENTURY EUROPE

June to Alice: You and I are both on the family tree I grew up with.
Alice: I did not grow up in Europe with a family tree, I grew up with cousins. We knew who was who, and that was our social circle in Vienna. Once a year when I was little, we travelled to Slovakia to visit the Mandl family or to Poland to see the Glasgall family.
Alice Glasgall Gingold (1924–2014), New Jersey 2009.

While all of Yetty Werner Mandl's siblings migrated to the U.S. by 1895, her husband Jacob's nine siblings remained in Europe. The sons and daughters of Lazar and Therese Mandl thrived in various locations and professions throughout the Austro–Hungarian Empire. All married and had children. The oldest, Marie Mandl, married physician Jonas Schlafrig, and raised six children in Mistelbach, Austria. Bernhard "Beni" Mandl was a scholar and principal of a Jewish secondary school in Budapest, Hungary. Two Mandl brothers had businesses in Vienna—Josef (book binding) and David (hat manufacturing). Simon was a rabbi in Neutitschein, Moravia (Czech Republic) and Heinrich a physician in Slovakia.

During the first half of the 20th century, the Mandl clan remained close. In Vienna, they gathered in each other's homes, often for piano and violin recitals. They traveled regularly to visit with those not nearby and vacationed together at lakeside resorts. Josef Mandl's daughter Paula Mandl Pentley (1896–1957), in a memoir written in

Australia where she had emigrated in the 1930's, recalled a visit to her uncle Jonas Schlafrig's home in Mistelbach, Austria, providing a rare glimpse of the patriarch Lazar Mandl. Paula wrote:

In the days when the new century was only a few years old and Hitler not yet erupted by the convulsions of history, Mistelbach seemed to me, born and reared in a big city [Vienna], as a thing out of a storybook—not quite real but very pleasant. Driving in a sledge through high snow to my uncle's [Jonas Schlafrig's] home from the station, the marketplace we passed was a thoroughly plain and uneventful affair and no phantasy was vivid enough to visualize this same place as the centre of a hysterical mob, women to a great part, shouting slogans with voices pitched high with frenzy, milling round and round to get a view of the beloved "Feuhrer," wishdream and idol of millions of frustrated and sentimental nonentities. No, at this time it was plain, slightly boring and in its slow—motion activities rather funny compared with the haste and variety of a big city.

My uncle's home was a typical small town place, two widespread one—storey wings enclosing a big "Hof": piled up timber on one side, that gave a most romantic setting for our plays of gendarme and robber, grocer and customer and similar pastimes. The other side of the "Hof" was still more romantic for a city child: the stable with horse and buggy (my uncle was a physician) and the chicken coop where, by some particular kindness of nature, there were nearly always tiny chickens running round just when we came for our habitual visit. One of our beloved duties was to catch maikaefer [beetles] in the adjoining vegetable garden with its beautiful old fruit trees, maikaefer being a special treat for the older chickens, that caused hectic fights among them.

My uncle was a very special kind of person in our eyes with his kind and manly looking face, his high forehead and snow—white hair in a circle round his bare skull. Our phantasy was spurred by the fact that he had been a "Feldscher" [army surgeon] in the Franco—Prussian War and then he was growing cactus—two good reasons to impress a city child. A man who had actually been in a war! Though none of us was really quite sure what "having been in a war" meant. But it sounded so very interesting. And then the cactus—a whole window full with most unusual and astonishing shapes—we just stood and stared.

The highlight of the day came with the meal with the grownups, sitting on one of those backbreaking chairs with the enormously high, straight back, all carved and polished in nutbrown wood; sitting at the large family table that was presided by a wonderful old man with grey beard and a little black velvet skull cap on his longish grey hair and beautiful dark kind eyes: grandfather [Lazar Mandl], who wanted to know what we last had [learned?] in biblical history and who seemed to know all about it.

A charming place where I had my first "best friend," a little girl with the poetic name of "Mimi Regen" and I was even allowed to play with her though she was only the daughter of uncle's factotum. A very unusual thing to be allowed—democracy was not yet the catch-cry. I wonder if Mimi Regen was one of the frenzied women, pouring all their not-fulfilled wishes in the cry: "Wir wollen unseren Fuehrer! Heil Hitler!"

Lazar Mandl 1817–1903   Paula Mandl (Pentley) 1896–1957

The European Mandls also stayed in touch with their brother Jacob in New York. In 1915, the youngest sibling, David, sent Jacob this postcard greeting with a photo of brothers Bernhard and David with their wives and children.

David wrote on the postcard (English translation):

My dear ones,

For the upcoming Rosh Hashanah holiday, we are sending you our best wishes! May your prayers be fulfilled! On Dec. 14, we will visit the graves of our parents [Lazar & Therese Mandl] of blessed memory and there we will also think of you.

From time to time we get telegraphic writings and good news from our dear Albert [Schlafrig, a physician with the Austrian Army during WWI.]

In the name of everyone, Sincerely David.

Seated: Clara Schlafrig Mandl, Bernhard, Ester Keleti Mandl, David. Rear: Richard, Ottilie, (children of Clara and David) Sara, Raphael (children of Bernhard and first wife Jenny Ehrenwald)

In addition to Albert Schlafrig, several other Mandls served in the Austrian army during World War I, including Albert's younger brother Gustav Schlafrig, David Mandl and two of his nephews, Eduard Mandl (son of Johanna and Herman Mandl) and Robert (son of Josef and Friederike Mandl, brother of Paula).

David Mandl 1871–1945   Eduard Mandl 1894–1943

Robert Mandl, serving in the cavalry, was shot in the foot in battle. In January 1915 he sent this photo postcard to Jacob Mandl in New York:

Robert Mandl indicated by arrow far right.

The text of the postcard [English translation] reads:

Dear Uncle,

Thank you again for your dear greetings. I congratulate you with all my heart for arrival of your new grandchild [Eleanor Goldberger, born in New York, Oct. 23, 1914]. I am sending you a picture from the hospital in which I am being sheltered. I am already much improved and beginning to walk. It also looks like there will not be lasting damage.

Robert was decorated with an Iron Cross, which he brought along when he emigrated to Australia in the 1930's, escaping the Nazi takeover of Austria.

Robert Mandl 1889–1949

Following World War I, the next generations of Mandls came of age, entering professions and businesses, and beginning families of their own. Family visits and summer holidays together continued, providing fond memories well into the next century. David Mandl's grandchildren Charles and Marianne Winter of Vienna, and Bernhard Mandl's granddaughter Zsuzsanna Frank, who lived with her parents and grandparents in Budapest, spent time together in the 1930s at summer resorts in Bled, Slovenia, Voslau, Austria and Lake Balaton in Hungary. Charlie Winter recalled that, "Zsuzsa and my sister Marianne and I played and swam together. I remember [Bernhard] spent the whole summer reading." In 1934, Bernhard wrote to his brother David in Vienna from the Lake Balaton, Hungary, resort owned and run by a Jewish Teachers' Union. Bernhard wrote:

Our spa treatment consists of food, sleep, and movement. Eszti [Bernhard's wife], in order to lose weight, takes a daily walk into the health resort in the morning. I, on the other hand, like the cat with its mousing, cannot leave off from writing.... We have ... a view of the very nearby mountains and very good orthodox–kosher food.

Zsuzsa recalled relatives from Czechoslovakia, Austria, Hungary, and Germany coming for visits, mostly to see her much–esteemed grandfather.

Marianne Winter on summer holiday with,
l–r: her parents Ottilie & Friedrich Winter, and uncle Richard Mandl, 1934

In the 20th century, secular secondary education became the norm, and university education, especially for the boys, became more common. Albert Schlafrig's son Otto followed him into medicine. By the 1920's, two of Albert's brothers, Friedrich and Gustav Schlafrig, were successful architects, married and raising children in Vienna. Gustav Schlafrig and his wife Josepha Kammellander had a daughter, Helga. Friedrich and his wife Fanny Witovsky, twin sister of Albert's wife Lina, had two children—Wilhelm and Marie.

l–r: Albert, Lina, Gustav, Otto Schlafrig, David Mandl, Robert Schlafrig, Vienna ca. 1930

Five of the Schlafrigs are included in an encyclopedia of 20th century Viennese architects and designers. *In Wien Erbaut (Built in Vienna)*[1] has biographical entries for Friedrich, Gustav, Wilhelm, Marie, and Robert Schlafrig.

In 1908, brothers Gustav and Friedrich Schläfrig designed the apartment building at Dannebergplatz 9 in Vienna where both lived for a time. After serving as a reserve officer in the Austrian army during the First World War, Gustav became head architect of a railway workers' housing cooperative. As leader of the cooperative and in his private practice, Gustav planned numerous housing complexes in Vienna and the Austrian federal provinces. He was an acknowledged expert in the field of social housing.

Gustav Schlafrig 1881–1950

Dannebergplatz 9, Vienna,
designed by Gustav and Friedrich Schlafrig

Friedrich "Fritz" Schlafrig was an architectural engineer and official in the Austrian Federal Railways. His avocation was the construction of violins and study of acoustics of wooden instruments. Cousins Wilhelm and Robert Schlafrig graduated with degrees in architecture from the Technical University in Vienna in the early 1930s and started a firm together. Marie Schlafrig received a diploma in art and design in 1931.

Friedrich "Fritz" Schlafrig 1875–1953

Fanny Witovsky Schlafrig 1886–1965

Wilhelm Schlafrig (William Shaw) 1909–1970   Marie Schlafrig (Frotten) 1911–2011

Careers and higher education were not widely available to women in early 20th century Europe; differing expectations for men and women prevailed in the Mandl family as well. Nonetheless, several of Lazar and Therese Mandl's granddaughters were professional teachers, including Bernhard Mandl's daughter Sara Frank in Budapest, and music teachers Louise Schlafrig Friedmann, and Ottilie Mandl Winter in Vienna. Melitta Aschkenes, who remained unmarried, was a scholar and teacher of English language and literature. She had studied in England and was head of the English special group at the Volksheim Ottakring (Institute of Adult Education in Vienna). With regard to her work there during World War I, Melitta was described as "the tried and tested chairwoman" who taught with "undiminished selfless zeal."[2]

Notes

1 Helmut Weihsmann, *In Wien erbaut, Lexikon der Wiener Architekten des 20. Jahrhunderts* (2005).

2 Wilhelm Filla, *Miss AS Levetus: A Cross Border Popular Educator*, Journal for the History of Adult Education and Science Popularization, pp. 24–39 (2001).

Mandl and Aschkenes Cousins in Chapter 8

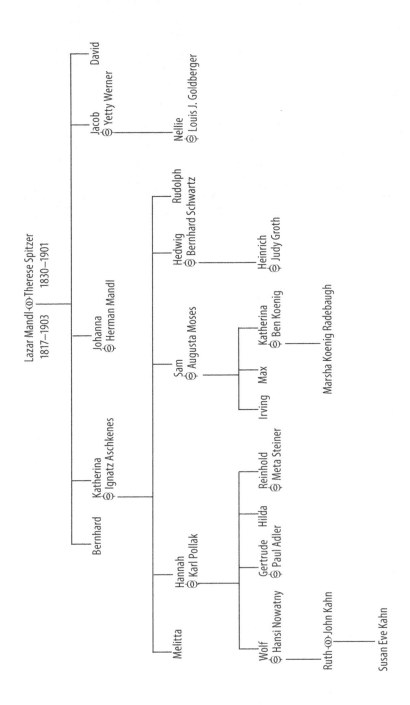

8.

JACOB MANDL'S 1912 LETTER
TO MELITTA ASCHKENES

The second Mandl daughter, Katherina, married a cantor, Ignatz Aschkenes. Sadly, Katherina died in 1892 when she gave birth to her fifth child at age 38. After Ignatz died in 1911, their oldest child, Melitta, sought assistance from her uncle Jacob Mandl for her brother Schaum "Sam" who hoped to emigrate to the U.S. Although German was the native language of both uncle and niece, Melitta was a teacher of English in Vienna, so they corresponded in English. Jacob's letter to Melitta is dated Feb. 9, 1912:

My dear Niece:

We were pleased to read your letters of recent date and as the matter concerning Schaum needs immediate attention I hasten to send you my answer.

[...]

I certainly do think that he will find work here, but he will have to accept it in whatever form it offers itself. 'The looser can't be the chooser.' Yet I will do my very best and try to find for him something suitable, after I have seen what he is best fit for.

Of course I will lend him a helping hand by way of recommending him to some decent, and as you say 'inexpensive but respectable' house. He won't have far to go. Did you really think that your Uncle and Aunt are mean enough to see the son of their late lamented sister arrive in this country and not keep their home wide open for him? We live very modestly and he will have to be satisfied with what we offer him; and if it pleases him to stay with us, and he begins to earn enough, I presume he will be glad to contribute toward his support.

[....]

Notify me as soon as he bought the ticket by what line and steamer he comes. Either myself or Aunty will be there to meet him. [...] If by any chance we should fail to be on time in meeting him on arrival he should send at once telegraphic message. Let him make a note of my address several times, so that in case he loses one he will be sure to get me.

I also wish that you would make up your mind to come over here, and give me an opportunity to find for you a good husband who would know how to appreciate your excellent qualities.

[....]

Affectionately,

Uncle Jacob

Jacob's letter includes travel instructions for Sam. He should book passage on a North German Lloyd or Hamburg–American steamship as "Rotterdam and Antwerp boats are not clean." Sam must have $40 with him at landing "to show the immigrant is provided for immediate wants." He should be careful with his money and "keep away from suspicious looking people."

Jacob asks Melitta for two favors. Jacob's brother David Mandl had a landlord in Vienna who manufactured ostrich plumes. Jacob requests, "If it is not very inconvenient," that Melitta see Uncle David about obtaining some for him. Finally, Jacob tells Melitta the happy news that his daughter Cornelia "Nellie" Mandl was soon to marry Louis J. Goldberger. Jacob asks that Melitta contact his sister Johanna Mandl in Ostra,[1] who has a wedding present of some bedding for Nellie that Sam could bring along as baggage.

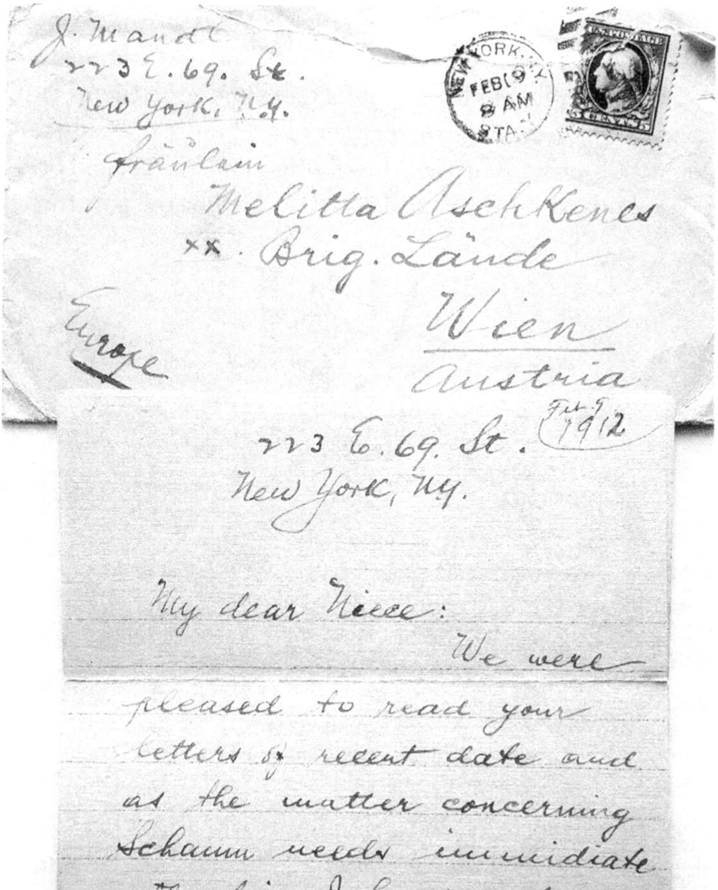

J. Mandl
223 E. 69. St.
New York, N.Y.

Fräulein
Melitta Aschkenes
xx . Brig. Lände
Wien
Austria
Europe

223 E. 69. St.   Feb. 9
New York, N.Y.   1912

My dear Niece:
            We were
pleased to read your
letters of recent date and
as the matter concerning
Schaum needs immidiate
attention I hasten to send
you my answer.
    I asked also received a
letter from Schaum and
will answer it tomorrow,
as it is getting rather
late tonight.
    And now I will answer
your questions and gladly
give you the informations

Jacob Mand's letter to niece Melitta Aschkenes 1912

Aboard the S.S. President Grant (Hamburg–American Line) in March 1912, Sam Aschkenes, age 28, met Emanuel and Regina Moses, who were traveling with two young daughters. The Moses family was emigrating to New York where their older children already resided. A daughter, Augusta "Gussie" Moses, single and age 28, had been living in New York with her married sister's family for the past three years.

Sam Aschkenes, top rear, enroute to New York, 1912

Sam Aschkenes and Gussie Moses married in 1913. They raised three children—Irving, Mac, and Katherina—in the Bronx, New York. Sam's 1920 application for U.S. citizenship was witnessed by his uncle Jacob Mandl and his cousin Nellie's husband Louis J. Goldberger.

Sam and Gussie Moses Aschkenes, 1914

Melitta Aschkenes, 1905

Sam worked in the garment industry, and was an amateur artist, enjoying both drawing and painting. In the mid–1950s, Sam turned the Mandl family genealogy, compiled by his uncle Bernhard "Beni" Mandl in Budapest, into the tree that appears at the beginning of this book. Sam drew the tree as a gift for his cousin, Nellie Mandl Goldberger.

Cousins Sam Aschkenes and Nellie Mandl Goldberger,
at Louis and Nellie's 40th wedding anniversary celebration, Brooklyn, NY, March 1952

Melitta never did take her Uncle Jacob up on his suggestion that he find her a husband in America. In May 1940, however, escaping the Nazi regime in Vienna, Melitta finally joined her brother Sam in America. Melitta brought with her Jacob Mandl's 1912 letter, which she sent to Nellie Goldberger in 1960, along with a note: "Here is the letter I told you about, written by your dear father 48 years ago."

Two of Melitta and Sam's sisters—Hanna Aschkenes Pollak and Hedwig Aschkenes Schwartz—and several nieces and nephews also managed to emigrate to the U.S. from Nazi–occupied Austria. In March 1941, Melitta wrote to her uncle David Mandl, who had arrived in New York from Vienna the same month as Melitta:

It is with joy that I am able to tell you that Hedwig and Bernhard [Schwartz, Hedwig's husband] arrived here Monday morning in good health! However, they didn't have such a calm trip over as we did, but now they are, praise God, here!… One really has no idea what is going on there.

Some years later, Melitta's nephew Wolf Pollak noted that many of the relatives learned English from Melitta in Vienna, a great blessing when they arrived in the U.S.

Marsha Koenig Radebaugh, born in 1946, loved childhood visits with her Great–Aunt Melitta, who showed her beautiful big "coffee table" books filled with photos of Vienna. Marsha commented that studying German in high school, she would hear Melitta's voice in her head: "Her German was so beautiful, as was her English and demeanor in general."

Aschkenes Descendants Born in Europe, Safe in America, ca.1948
Standing: Rheinhold and Meta Steiner Pollak, Paul Adler,
Henry and Judy Groth Schwartz, Wolf Pollak, Melitta Aschkenes
Seated: Bernhard and Hedwig Aschkenes Schwartz, Hilda Pollak, Hansi Nowotny Pollak
(front), Susan Eve Kahn

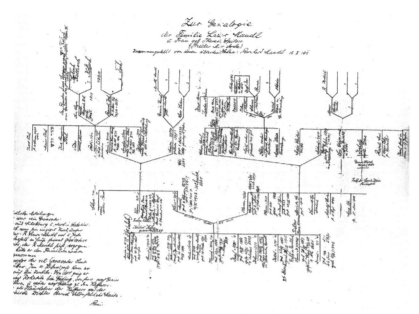

Mandl–Spitzer Genealogy in German and Hebrew compiled by Bernhard Mandl in 1911,
source for the Mandl–Spitzer Family Tree that Sam Aschkenes created in 1952
for Nellie Mandl Goldberger. (See Preface.)
Originals of this Genealogy and a progeny chart compiled in the 1930s
are located in the David Mandl Collection, Leo Baeck Institute, NY.

Notes

1 Johanna Mandl and her husband Hermann lived in Uherske Ostroh,
Moravia, where they owned a distillery producing slivovitz, a plum wine.

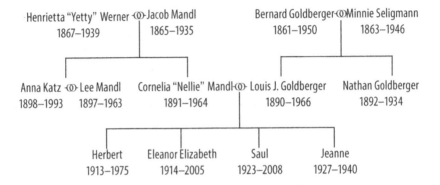

Henrietta "Yetty" Werner ⟨∞⟩ Jacob Mandl   Bernard Goldberger ⟨∞⟩ Minnie Seligmann
        1867–1939   1865–1935   1861–1950   1863–1946

Anna Katz ⟨∞⟩ Lee Mandl   Cornelia "Nellie" Mandl ⟨∞⟩ Louis J. Goldberger   Nathan Goldberger
1898–1993   1897–1963   1891–1964   1890–1966   1892–1934

        Herbert   Eleanor Elizabeth   Saul   Jeanne
        1913–1975   1914–2005   1923–2008   1927–1940

9.

LOU AND NELLIE MANDL GOLDBERGER—
FEAST AND FAMINE

In 1902, Bernard and Minnie Seligmann Goldberger took their two sons, Louis Joseph and Nathan, to Europe for three months of travel and visits with German relatives. The following year, Lou celebrated his Bar Mitzvah in New York, city of his birth.[1] As befitted a New York congregation of German–speaking immigrants like his parents, Lou delivered English and German Bar Mitzvah speeches. In remarks both pious and patriotic, Louis declared,

> *It shall further be my determination to live in purity and chastity, to live and to die an Israelite, and to live and to die in my ancestral faith. May my heart also be filled with love and patriotism for my native land, always be a true observer of American principles as adopted by our great Republic to be one of the admirers of Liberty and Equality. May I grow up a useful Member of society, a thankful servant to the Most High God.*

Louis J Goldberger Bar Mitzvah speech in English and German, 1903

Fluency in German would prove useful in Lou's professional life and later on when he and Nellie brought into their Brooklyn home a stream of family members escaping the European Holocaust.

Nine years after his bar mitzvah, Lou married Cornelia "Nellie" Mandl, also the child of German–speaking immigrants. Nellie was born in Wessely, Moravia, near Vienna, and came to the U.S. with her parents at age two in 1893.

Cornelia "Nellie" Mandl, 1912   Louis J. Goldberger, 1912

Mr. and Mrs. Jacob Mandl

and

Mr. and Mrs. Bernard Goldberger

beg to announce the marriage

of their children

Cornelia

to

Louis Joseph

on Sunday, the twenty-fourth of March,

nineteen hundred and twelve.

At Home

April twenty-first and twenty-eighth

From
3 to 6 p.m.

323 Lincoln Road
Brooklyn

Wedding announcement and invitation, March 24, 1912

As it was for most of the country, the 1920s, 30s, and 40s were years of boom and bust, prosperity and hardship for Lou and Nellie. After high school, Lou entered the retail linen trade in New York. At the height of his business success in the 1920s, Lou travelled by ocean liner to Europe once or twice a year, several weeks at a time, purchasing fine linens and other luxury goods for import to the U.S. In addition to bringing home European items for his own household, Lou on one occasion arrived home with a Doberman named Axel and on another a German shepherd named Alf. Nellie managed the household in Brooklyn, which grew to include four children, Lou's parents, and a live–in housemaid.

Louis J. Goldberger, Venice, Italy, 1926

Louis J. Goldberger aboard ship with Axel

Eleanor, Saul, Nellie, Herbert Goldberger, 1926

The family's prosperity was on display at oldest child Herbert's Bar Mitzvah in 1926.

Seated, l to r: Bernard and Minnie Goldberger, Henrietta "Yetty" Werner Mandl, Eleanor and Nellie Goldberger, Anna Katz (Mrs. Lee) Mandl.
Standing l to r: Jacob Mandl, Herbert and Louis J. Goldberger, Lee Mandl

Like other New Yorkers of means, the Goldbergers were able to send Eleanor to summer camp in the mountains. Eleanor considered her three summers at Camp Rondack in the Adirondacks as some of the happiest times of her life. This was so even though one summer began with a memorable auto accident on the way to camp. The Goldberger's chauffeur was driving their Franklin automobile with Nellie Goldberger in the front seat, and housemaid Mary Lenart in the back seat with 12–year–old Eleanor and 3–year–old Saul, when they collided with another vehicle that had skidded on the wet road. Fortunately, injuries, mostly caused by flying glass, were not serious.

FOUR INJURED WHEN AUTOMOBILE SKIDS

Four persons were injured yesterday afternoon when the automobile in which they were riding, collided with another machine on the Waterford-Mechanicville road about two miles north of Waterford. The injured, all residents of Brooklyn, are in the Cohoes Hospital, where they are being attended for bruises and cuts about the face and body. Their injuries are not serious, it was said.

The injured are Mrs. Louise Goldberger, her daughter Eleanor 12, her son, Saul, 3, and, Miss Mary Lenart. They are being attended by Dr. F. J. Scott of Waterford.

The car in which they were riding was driven by David Renier of Brooklyn, the Goldberger's chauffeur, and was on its way towards Saratoga, when another machine driven by William Houseman of Chatham, skidded on the wet pavement. Houseman was accompanied by his wife. Neither was injured.

Both automobiles were sedans and the occupants of the Goldberger machine were cut by the flying glass. The chauffeur, Renier, was not injured.

Goldbergers' Franklin sedan post-accident

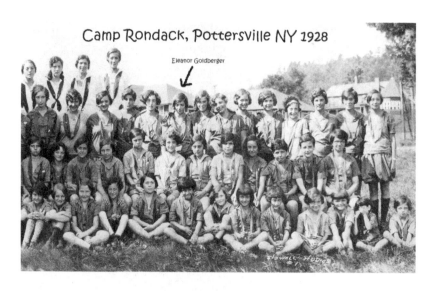

Camp Rondack, Pottersville NY 1928

Eleanor Goldberger

Nellie gave birth to her fourth child, Jeanne, while Lou was sailing home from Europe aboard the S.S. Columbus in 1927. The event was noted on the ship's dining menu that evening.

To my TINY and her
Wonderful MOTHER

———

L. G. Goldberger
and Party

MENU

Malossol Caviare

Soup Dubarry

Boiled Rhine Salmon, Sauce Riche

Bresse Poularde
New Peas, Bartlett Pears
Roman Salad with French Dressing

Mocha Ice Cream, Petits Fours

Fruits   Cheese   Coffee

S.S. »COLUMBUS«   Wednesday, June 1st 1927

On this occasion, Lou brought home "Schwester," a proper German baby nurse to care for the infant.

Jeanne Goldberger, 1928   "Schwester" Anne Marie Stellmach

Then everything changed. By 1930, Lou's businesses were failing. Political and economic conditions in Europe were deteriorating, the stock market crashed in 1929, and the Great Depression began. The availability in Europe, and the demand in the U.S., for expensive household goods largely disappeared. In addition, in the 1920s and 1930s Lou was the sole breadwinner not only for Nellie and their children, but he also supported his parents and helped support Nellie's parents and her sister Stella Mandl.

By 1933 when Eleanor graduated from high school, Lou's import business had declared bankruptcy, restarted, and declared bankruptcy again. Both Herbert and Eleanor entered the workforce soon after high school graduation. An additional setback occurred when Lou was injured in an accident. He suffered a fractured skull when a jack slipped while he was working under his car at home in Brooklyn. While Lou recovered, his resources were depleted. After declaring personal bankruptcy in 1935, Lou rebuilt his business, this time as a broker in the domestic textile trade. Adolf Hitler's rise to power in Germany meant not only the end of Lou Goldberger's European business, but would create new concerns for the lives and welfare of aunts, uncles, and cousins across the Atlantic.

Notes

1 Lou's Bar Mitzvah was celebrated at Congregation Shaare Zedek of Harlem, third oldest congregation in New York City.

Mandls and Nathans in Chapter 10

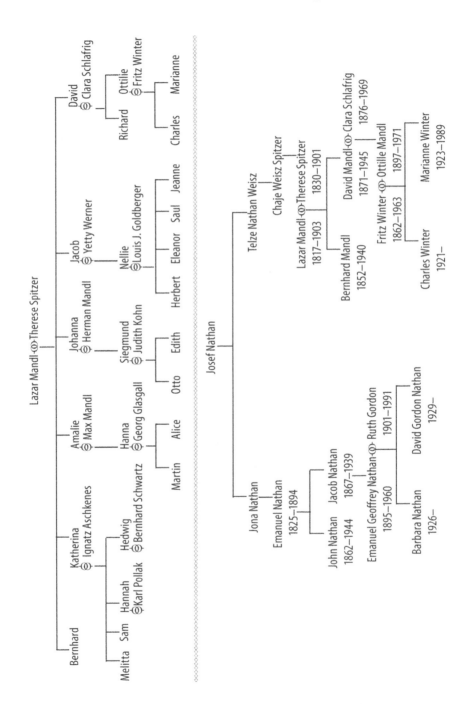

10.

COMING TO AMERICA:
ESCAPING THE HOLOCAUST

L ife for Jews in Central Europe was increasingly difficult with the rise of Nazi Germany in the 1930's. To escape persecution, our remaining European family members sought to emigrate. The fortunate ones found havens in England, the U.S., South Africa and Australia.

The situation in Vienna became dire with the Anschluss—Nazi Germany's annexation of Austria—in March 1938. Jews were no longer allowed to attend school or practice professions outside of Jewish institutions. The government began confiscating Jewish businesses and property. Germany imposed enormous barriers to emigration. Necessary documents were expensive and included identity paperwork, police certificates, exit and transit permissions, and others. Those leaving were allowed to take only a small amount of cash.

Obtaining an immigrant visa to the U.S. required an Affidavit of Support—a document from a U.S. citizen promising to be financially responsible for the immigrant and showing sufficient income and assets to do so. Deep into the Depression, U.S. relatives, flooded with pleas for assistance, could not provide Affidavits for all those needing them. Help was sought from relief organizations (B'nai B'rith, HIAS, JDC[1]), distant relatives, and even complete strangers.

In Brooklyn New York, Lou and Nellie Mandl Goldberger managed to obtain Affidavits of Support for two Mandl boys in Vienna—Otto Mandl, grandson of Nellie's aunt Johanna Mandl, and Karl Winter, grandson of Nellie's uncle David Mandl. On July 16, 1938, Nellie wrote:

> Dear Uncle David, Am glad to write to you that the affidavit was delivered today to the Cunard White Star Line ... Mr. Maurice Ullman signed the affidavit. He is my son Herbert's father-in-law. ... Please have Cousin Winter [Karl's father Friedrich Winter] get in touch with Sigmund Mandl as his son Otto Mandl is on the same affidavit. . . Also please try and have enough clothes for Karl for possibly two years, as we are not financially able to clothe them. However, will try and make Karl happy, and he will feel this is his home.[2]

Sixteen-year-old Otto and seventeen-year-old Karl (known as Charles or Charlie in the U.S.) came to live with the Goldbergers in Brooklyn in late 1938. The Goldbergers' efforts and generosity enabled Charlie's parents, Friedrich and Ottilie Winter, to emigrate in September 1939, and his uncle Richard Winter in November 1939. Charlie's grandparents David and Clara Schlafrig Mandl arrived in February 1940, as did Otto's parents and younger sister, Siegmund, Judith, and Edith Mandl.

Otto Mandl's exit from Vienna was particularly memorable. Otto's father Siegmund was employed in a Jewish-owned bank. After the Anschluss in March 1938, the Nazis "aryanized" the firm, assigning management to a non-Jewish employee. In September 1938, while Siegmund was arranging for the family's emigration, the situation became urgent. Years later, Otto recalled someone warning Siegmund that his name was on a list to be arrested,[3] while his sister Edith remembered a neighbor threatening the family.[4] Both, of course, may have been the case. On very short notice, therefore, Siegmund, Judith, Otto, and Edith, along with Judith's sister and her family,[5] boarded a train out of Vienna, ending up in Brussels, Belgium, where HIAS provided them with refugee lodgings.

Despite the Affidavit the Goldbergers had sent in July, visas for Otto and Charlie were not yet available at the U.S. Embassy in Vienna when the Mandls departed in September. Inquiring at the embassy in Belgium, Siegmund was told that Otto must return to Vienna for his visa. So 16–year–old Otto Mandl journeyed alone to Nazi Vienna where for several weeks he moved around the city to avoid detection, checking each day at the U.S. Embassy for the visa. The new manager of Siegmund's bank, who knew Otto, permitted him to withdraw money from Siegmund's remaining funds. Otto used his pockets full of cash to bribe his way out of close calls with German and Austrian police who were harassing and randomly arresting Jews. At one point, he was arrested and placed on a truck, but jumped off as it started to move, and escaped. Another time, Otto simply threw a fistful of bills at his assailants, and ran away. Otto converted some of the cash into objects he might be able to transport to America past the Nazi confiscators—gold fountain pens and suits of clothing. He would be a well–appointed refugee! Otto finally left Vienna on November 9, 1938—Kristallnacht.[6] He boarded the Queen Mary in Cherbourg France on November 12, landing in New York five days later.

Otto Mandl and Lou Goldberger met Charlie Winter at the dock when he arrived in New York a few weeks after Otto. When Nellie Goldberger died in 1964, Charlie wrote to Lou Goldberger,

> *I will always remember Aunt Nellie as the wonderfully kind, patient and understanding woman who 25 years ago made your house a real home for me. In retrospect, now that I have youngsters of my own of almost that age, I realize just how difficult having 2 boys 17 years old thrust into your midst must have been for you both. Yet, you never had anything but good humor and encouragement for us.*

Lou Goldberger, however, was not one to coddle his new charges. Otto Mandl remembered "Uncle Louis" as a demanding patriarch with high standards and strict expectations for his family. Otto recalled that the day after his arrival, Uncle Louis told him that until he found outside employment, Otto would be expected to come with him to the office each morning, to help in whatever way he could. He was also tasked, along with Lou's teenage son Saul, to keep the family car cleaned, waxed, and shining. Lou concluded this announcement by saying, "And this, Otto, is the last conversation we will have in German. We speak only English from now on."

Otto Mandl and the Goldbergers' car, at home, 1929 63rd St. Brooklyn, NY, 1939

Lou doled out lunch money to Otto each day, but Lou's daughter, 24–year–old Eleanor, feared that it was not sufficient for a growing boy's needs. She would often slip a sandwich into his coat pocket as he headed out the door with her father in the morning. Eleanor Goldberger also escorted her two newly–arrived teenage cousins to New York's Times Square on New Year's Eve to welcome in 1939.

Charles Winter, Eleanor Goldberger, Otto Mandl, 1939, Brooklyn, NY

It was not until fourteen months after Otto arrived in New York that his parents and sister—Siegmund, Judith and Edith—left Belgium for New York. At one point, HIAS, the agency sheltering the family, was sufficiently overwhelmed with refugees that they arranged to send the Mandls to Czechoslovakia. Siegmund's mother Johanna and brother Eduard lived in the Czech town of Uherske Ostroh, and Siegmund, having been born there, had a Czech passport. When Judith saw the train tickets that had been purchased for them, however, she realized that the travel date—October 4, 1938—would be Yom Kippur. Judith balked at traveling on that holy day, telling Siegmund to notify HIAS that the trip would be impossible. Siegmund was embarrassed, but Judith insisted, "They are Jews, they will understand." Before another travel date was arranged, Nazi Germany took over Czechoslovakia, and it was no longer a viable option for the Mandls. Tragically, Johanna, Eduard, and Eduard's wife Meda did not survive the war.[7]

In February 1940, Otto met Siegmund, Judith and Edith at the Port of New York. Also there to greet them was Siegmund's first cousin Sam Aschkenes, who himself had been met at the port by their uncle Jacob Mandl in 1912. (See Chapter 8.) Siegmund and family lived with Nellie and Lou Goldberger for six weeks before moving into an apartment of their own. Siegmund, a university–educated banker, went to work in the tool and die shop where his son Otto worked, a situation that was awkward for them both. Judith, an accomplished seamstress, found work as a dressmaker.

For 12–year–old Edith, the transition, especially the time with the Goldbergers, was difficult. Edith recalled many years later that her first night in America, February 3, 1940, she was given the room of a girl her same age who had recently died. Lou and Nellie Goldberger's youngest child, 12–year–old Jeanne, was diagnosed with bone cancer in the Spring of 1939. Edith's cousin Jeanne died at home on January 25, 1940.

Jeanne Goldberger, 1939

Moreover, Edith had been very happy at her school in Brussels, where the teachers were kind and she became fluent in French. She had not learned very much English, however. When Lou Goldberger announced to the gathered family that Edith would begin to attend school the next day, Edith replied, "Nein!", to the great distress of her parents.

In January 1939, Charlie Winter's younger sister Marianne traveled alone from Vienna to New York, as he had done a month before. Marianne's

Edith Mandl, ca. 1945

path to the U.S., however, was quite different than her brother's.

Mr. Nathan, Soap Manufacturer, Boston MA

After Lou and Nellie Goldberger obtained the Affidavits of Support for Otto Mandl and Charlie Winter to come to the U.S., they had exhausted their resources. The Mandl family in Vienna continued to seek a way for Charlie's 15–year–old sister Marianne to emigrate along with her brother. As Charlie told the story:

Your grandparents [Lou and Nellie] had vouched for Otto's and my not becoming public burdens so that we could get immigration visas. Frantically trying to find someone who would vouch for my sister, Marianne, my grandfather, David Mandl, wrote to his brother, Bernhard Mandl in Budapest for suggestions. Uncle Beni remembered a distant relative by the name of Nathan in Boston, so, having almost finished three years of English in high school, I wrote to "Mr. Nathan, Soap Manufacturer, Boston, Massachusetts" and the letter got there, and the Nathans vouched for Marianne. She came to the US alone, not quite 16 years old, and lived with the Nathans for a few years while we were getting settled.

Marianne, Karl (Charles), and Ottilie Winter on holiday in Bled, Slovenia ,1937

The distant relative who remarkably received David Mandl's letter was Emanuel Geoffrey Nathan, whose grandfather Emanuel Nathan (1825–1894) came to the U.S. from Hungary in the mid–19th century and founded a textile soap business in Boston.[8] Emanuel Nathan was a first cousin of the Mandl siblings' grandmother Chaje Weisz Spitzer.

Geoffrey Nathan's response to the Mandls' letter came via Julius Kahn, a New York attorney who had been a close friend of David Mandl's late brother Jacob Mandl, Nellie Goldberger's father. Julius Kahn's letter, which arrived in August 1938, contained very good news:

Dear Mr. Mandl:

Mr. E. Geoffrey Nathan of 69 Prentiss Street, Boston, Mass., was kind enough to call upon me yesterday. At this time, I wish to thank you very much for making it possible for me to meet Mr. Nathan, whom I found to be a gentleman in every respect.

He has consented to undertake the responsibility of Miss Marianna Winter, sister of Charles Winter. I do not believe that the generosity of Mr. Nathan is based on any 'mishpocha' considerations. ... [T]he picture of Miss Marianna has evoked his interest and the interest of his entire family and they are ready and prepared to receive her as a member of their family. He is married and has two children of his own. I think Miss Marianna is a very fortunate person because I feel that she is falling into the lap of genteel, cultured, refined environment, in the city where the American democracy was created. The papers for her will be sent within a few days and you will hear from Mr. Nathan directly.

I think that next to Marianna, you personally have captivated him to no little extent. ... I can well understand his feelings, because to a very large extent, your brother [Jacob Mandl], whom I called Uncle Jack, captivated me personally, in the very same way. When he departed, something within me went with him and I think of him as one of the few persons who have left their impress upon me for all time, to my benefit. I do not know to what extent, however, he will be able to actually be of some assistance to you. However, he will take that up with you personally.

[...]

... between my father and myself, and one other uncle, we have so far undertaken guaranteeships actually for 24 persons, with 16 more promised. The reason that we have not executed papers for these 16 is

that we do not wish to jeopardize others. As soon as the others are through and passed, we will send for the other 16. Since then, there have been 8 more requests out of Vienna. ... We here are living in daily terror of the situation in Czecho–Slovakia. ... I don't know how much longer we can keep on going. We have adopted the theory that we will keep piling on until it breaks of its own force, although only Heaven knows what we will do with them when they get here.

You may not be fully informed about the immigration laws of the United States so I have thought it might be interesting to tell you this. At first the sons and then the daughters should come over, particularly those who can establish themselves quickly. Under the immigration laws, they have a right to bring their wives, children, and fathers and mothers over as preference cases. This situation is beyond the control of the Consul and is controlled entirely from Washington here. In fact, it is a different department of the government entirely. The cases under which you now operate come in the Consular service of the Department of State, whereas if children bring their fathers and mothers over, it comes under the Department of Labor. That is the way these things should be done, otherwise you people will be using up the quota numbers not to the best interests of the general welfare.

I am closing this letter, a copy of which I am sending to Mr. Nathan, and with congratulations to you upon your good fortune to find Mr. Nathan, either as a long–lost relation, but better still, as a friend.

Marianne Winter's German Passport

We cannot be certain how the letter addressed only to "Mr. Nathan, Soap Manufacturer, Boston Massachusetts" arrived in Geoffrey Nathan's hands, but it appears that the Nathan family had been prominent in Boston for a very long time. One story recalled by Geoffrey Nathan's daughter Barbara was that her great–grandfather, the Hungarian immigrant Emanuel Nathan, was appalled by the "No Irish Need Apply" restrictions he saw on help–wanted advertisements in Boston in the late 1800's. In protest, Emanuel Nathan specified "Only Irish Need Apply" for employment at his businesses.

There is support for this story, and for Emanuel Nathan's notoriety, in an 1885 *Boston Herald* newspaper article entitled "A Jewish Wedding." The article describes in great detail the elaborate wedding of Emanuel Nathan's youngest daughter Theresa. The event was attended by Mayor Hugh O'Brien, Boston's first Irish and Catholic mayor, who toasted the newlyweds at their reception.

Emanuel Nathan's sons John and Jacob continued the soap manufacturing company, known as Roxbury Chemical Works, into the 20th century. They and their wives, Sarah and Lena, were also active in civic and philanthropic organizations. From 1907 to 1943, John Nathan was President of Temple Ohabei Shalom in Boston, the oldest Jewish congregation (founded 1842) and first synagogue built in Massachusetts, and second oldest in New England. In the 1920's, Temple Ohabei Shalom built an opulent edifice in suburban Brookline.

Temple Ohabei Shalom, Brookline ,MA

Upon his death in 1944, the *Boston Herald* described John Nathan as, "businessman and philanthropist known to thousands as 'Uncle John.'" When Jacob and Lena's son, Geoffrey Nathan, married Ruth Gordon in 1925, a *Boston Herald* article observed, "The wedding is of great interest to social circles in Brookline and Boston, where Miss Gordon and Mr. Nathan have been prominent." Perhaps it is not surprising after all that David Mandl's 1938 minimally–addressed letter found its way to Geoffrey Nathan.

Charlie Winter and Geoffrey Nathan met Marianne Winter in New York when she arrived from Vienna in January 1939. She lived in Boston with Geoffrey and Ruth Nathan until 1943, growing up with their children, David and Barbara. It is further likely that the Nathans were instrumental in the successful emigration of the older family members, particularly Charlie and Marianne's grandparents David and Clara Schlafrig Mandl. An Affidavit of Support for David and Clara Mandl was executed in December 1938 by a Cambridge,

First page of the Affidavit of Support for David and Clara Mandl

Massachusetts businessman who stated, "Although I am not related to said aliens, I have been induced to take a very strong interest in them through mutual friends."

Charlie and Marianne Winter's parents, Fritz and Ottilie Mandl Winter, arrived in New York in the Fall of 1939. Fritz, who like many of the Mandls was multi–lingual and had also traveled extensively as an executive of the Austrian National Railway, found work with an import–export firm, while Ottilie was able to continue teaching piano in the U.S.

Ottilie's parents, David and Clara Schlafrig Mandl, ages 69 and 64, arrived from Vienna in February 1940. Three months later, they attended the wedding of Lou and Nellie Goldberger's daughter Eleanor. In the wedding banquet photo, David and Clara are seated next to Maurice Ullmann, the Goldberger in–law who executed affidavits of support for several of the Mandls. It was customary at that time for those not attending a wedding to send congratulatory telegrams that were read aloud along with the speeches and toasts. One of those telegrams read at Eleanor's wedding is from Geoffrey and Ruth Nathan. Another has a note on the back in Nellie's handwriting: "Uncle David would like to say a few words." One can readily imagine the words of thanks David Mandl must have expressed to those in the room who engineered his and Clara's rescue along with their children, grandchildren, and so many others.

Wedding Dinner of Eleanor Goldberger and George Friedman. Standing, l–r: Lou and Nellie Goldberger, Eleanor, George, Riverside Plaza Hotel, New York, NY., May 26, 1940

David Mandl spent the next five years studying, writing, and seeking to be useful, especially to the Mandl relatives remaining in Europe. The David Mandl Collection at the Leo Baeck Institute in New York contains notebooks that David filled with writings in English about history and politics. There is correspondence seeking affidavits and assistance for Clara's brother Friedrich Schlafrig (see

Chapter 12) and David's niece Suzi Cires, (see Chapter 13) and their spouses, who remained in Europe, as well as correspondence with Mandls who had emigrated to the U.S., Australia, and South Africa. When he passed away in 1945, David was the last of the ten siblings born to Lazar and Therese Mandl in 19th century Senica, Slovakia.

Tante Hanna Glasgall and the Golden Child

When Otto Mandl was moving around Vienna trying to escape detection and looking for places to sleep in the Fall of 1938, he knocked on the door of his "Tante Hanna." Hanna Mandl Glasgall and Otto's father Siegmund were first cousins.[9] The two families, each with two children of similar ages, had been close social friends. Hanna and Georg Glasgall were married in Siegmund and Judith Mandl's apartment.

During those fraught days following the Anschluss, not all of Otto's contacts were happy to see a teenage boy who had slipped out and back into Vienna without authorization. Tante Hanna greeted him, however, with a hug and shout of "My golden child!" For the rest of his life, Otto remained grateful for the few days he spent in the Glasgall home being well fed and cared for.

When Otto arrived at the Glasgall apartment in October 1938, Hanna and Georg's own two children—Martin age 18 and Alice age 14—were already in the United States. Martin had been an exchange student in France, so in July 1938 the pair went first to his host family in Lyon. For protection, the two youngsters were accompanied to the train station in Vienna

Georg and Hanna Mandl Glasgall, Martin and Alice, 1928

by their non–Jewish neighbors. In August, Martin and Alice sailed from LeHarve to New York where they went to live with Glasgall cousins in Paterson, New Jersey. After Kristallnacht, the same non–Jewish neighbors helped keep Hanna and Georg out of sight in the basement of their apartment building until they were able to obtain visas and reunite with their children in the U.S. in March 1940.

Like the Mandls, our Werner relatives sought to escape Europe. On April 5, 1940, Eda Werner Perilstein wrote from Orrville Ohio to her niece Nellie Goldberger:

> *What are we going to do with all our new relatives who are pouring into New York? Julia Warner Peck wants 100 Dollars to bring out our cousin Leo Warner who with his family, wife and 2 beautiful grown up children are stranded refugees in China after a life of ease and luxury in Vienna.[10] Henry Herbatchek, your dear mother's [Yetty Werner Mandl] first cousin wants me to canvas this town for money to help Czechoslovakia's cause, and letters pouring in from the charity organizations from the large cities demanding money. It is heartbreaking not to have plenty of means to do for all! We will never forget your unselfishness to those forsaken people whom you took in.*

Post–War Lives

Adjusting to life in a new country with a new language was a challenge, perhaps easier for the teenagers than it was for their parents and grandparents. Charlie and Marianne Winter, Otto and Edith Mandl, Martin and Alice Glasgall all built lives that were a credit to the efforts and sacrifices of their elders, and to their own courage and perseverance.

Charlie Winter began attending college at night while working in various jobs in New York City. He enlisted in the US Army in 1942 and went to Europe with an Engineer Combat Battalion of the U.S. Seventh Army in1944. The Seventh Army distinguished itself in 1944 in difficult winter conditions during the Vosges Mountains campaign, clearing entrenched German forces from the west bank of the Rhine and stopping a German counteroffensive. The campaign marked the only contested advance through the Vosges Mountains ever to succeed. The Seventh Army then crossed the Rhine and fought its way across Germany from northwest to southeast,[11] entering Charlie's native Austria in April 1945, shortly before the war ended. Charlie's battalion was then assigned to occupation duties and, because his mother tongue was German, he was transferred to a military government unit in Hessen where he worked on political intelligence.

Discharged from the Army in 1946, Charlie earned an M.S. degree in Mechanical Engineering at Harvard University in 1948. Charlie worked for over 30 years at Sandia Labs in New Mexico, a government owned contractor that operated the part of the Atomic Energy Commission responsible for engineering atomic weapons. For 3 years in the 1960s, he served at AEC headquarters in Washington D.C. as Deputy Director of the Division of Military Applications (the nuclear weapons program). Charlie married Joan Finder, a refugee from Berlin, in 1947. Joan earned BA and MA degrees at the U. of New Mexico while raising their two children, William Winter and Ellen Winter Wiczer, and became a teacher of literature and German.

Marianne Winter earned a B.A. in Art from Hunter College in 1945 and a Masters in Social Work from the U. of Chicago in 1947. She married Richard Milton Martin in 1950 and earned a Ph.D. in Art History from Bryn Mawr in 1961. Richard's Ph.D. was in Mathematics and Metaphysics. Marianne taught at NYU, Bard College, Rutgers U. and Vassar College; she and Richard both taught in Europe as well. Richard became President of the American Metaphysical Society and Marianne was Chairman of the Fine Arts Department at Boston College and founder of the Boston College Art Gallery. Both Marianne and Richard were superb pianists.

Geoffrey and Ruth Nathan's son, David Gordon Nathan, M.D., who was ten years old when Marianne Winter arrived in their home, is a retired Professor at Harvard University Medical School and President Emeritus of the Dana Farber Cancer Institute at Boston Children's Hospital.

Otto Mandl served in the U.S. Army, but not overseas. After the war, he entered business as a broker of airplane parts. Otto and his wife Ina Schulman raised their two children in Baldwin, New York. Son David Mandl was a noted architect in New York City and daughter Susan Mandl a teacher and artist in Rochester, New York. David and Susan grew up surrounded by their grandfather Siegmund Mandl's drawings of urban European scenes and architecture. Although professionally a banker in Vienna, Siegmund was an accomplished artist, working primarily in pencil, reportedly because he was colorblind. His grandchildren were fortunate to inherit Siegmund's talent as well as his interest.

Siegmund Mandl's drawing of the
family's apartment building
at 13 Sterneckplatz
(now Max Winter Platz) in Vienna.

Edith Mandl (Hamberger) earned degrees from Hunter College and is a retired teacher of French and German on Long Island New York. Edith's husband Irving Hamberger was a teacher and professional photographer. Their son Richard and wife Carol have two daughters, Elizabeth and Caitlin.

Seated: Judith (Kohn) and Siegmund Mandl
Standing: Ina (Schulman), Otto and Edith Mandl, NY, 1946

Goldberger and Mandl Family Passover
Seated: Ina, Susan, Otto Mandl. Standing: Shirley, Barry, Jay, Anita, Saul Goldberger, David Mandl,
Edith Mandl Hamberger, Rick and Irving Hamberger, Baldwin NY, 1966.

Anita Boggia Mandl, Alan Friedman, Ina and Otto Mandl, June Entman,
David Mandl, Baldwin NY, 2005

Alice Glasgall married Sol Gingold, a pharmacist, in 1950. For the next 40+ years Alice raised their son Jeffrey and worked as a seamstress, department store buyer, and real estate salesperson, eventually opening her own real estate firm in New Jersey. In 1995, at age 71, Alice retired from her business and joined the U.S. Peace Corps. For two years, she served in the Peace Corps in Zvolen, Slovakia, teaching business skills at the local university. Her proudest achievement was raising funds and helping organize the restoration of a desecrated Jewish cemetery in Zvolen, which has become a Slovak national monument

Alice Glasgall Gingold at dedication of Holocaust
Memorial in Zvolen, Slovakia, 1998

honoring both Jews and non–Jews killed in the Holocaust. After the Peace Corps, Alice continued to work with the Jewish community in Zvolen, helping to revive Jewish life and practice there.

Martin Glasgall served on active duty in the U.S. Army from 1941 to 1945, becoming a U.S. citizen in 1942. For part of his time in the Army, Martin was stationed in the Canal Zone, Panama. At the end of 1947, Martin completed his B.A. degree at New York University, married Alice Ann Engholm, and the couple moved to Panama, where Martin went into the jewelry business, eventually selling jewelry and crystal throughout Latin America and the Carribean. Martin and Alice raised three children in Panama—Marsha Ann (Chisholm), Gary William, Lynn Alice (Eskilden).

Notes

1 HIAS = Hebrew Immigrant Aid Society; JDC = Joint Distribution Committee

2 Original in the David Mandl Collection, Leo Baeck Institute, NY.

3 2009 Interview with Otto Mandl, Baldwin NY.

4 Hamberger, Edith. Interview 23426. *Visual History Archive*, USC Shoah Foundation, 1996. In addition to Edith, our family members with recorded interviews in the Shoah Foundation Visual History Archive include Charlie and Joan Winter and Zsuzsanna Frank Turi (in Hungarian, see Chapter 12).

5 Judith's sister and nephew, Therese and Albert Reisz, perished in the Holocaust. Therese's husband and daughter, Jacob and Gertrude Reisz, arrived in the U.S. in 1948.

6 Kristallnacht, "Night of the Broken Glass" was two days of coordinated violence against Jews, Jewish businesses, homes, and houses of worship throughout Nazi Germany. In Vienna alone, almost all synagogues were destroyed, 27 Jews were murdered, 88 severely injured, and more than 6,500 arrested.

7 Johanna, Eduard, and Malvine (Meda) Falter Mandl were deported to concentration camps where they died in 1943.

8 Emanuel Nathan arrived in Philadelphia with wife Fanny and 3 young daughters around 1855. They later moved to Boston and had 4 more daughters and 2 sons.

9 Siegmund's mother Johanna Mandl and Hanna's mother Amalie Mandl were sisters, two of the ten Mandl siblings from Senica. See Chapter 1.

10 Leo Werner, 60–year–old watchmaker, his wife, son and daughter arrived in San Francisco from Shanghai on Sept. 21, 1940. Julia Warner Peck was the daughter of Lee S. Warner. See Chapter 2.

11 Unbeknownst to Charlie, when he was only about 15 miles away from Dachau, Germany, his cousin and childhood friend Zsuzsanna Frank (granddaughter of Bernhard Mandl) was hiding in the forest after escaping the Dachau concentration camp. See Chapter 12.

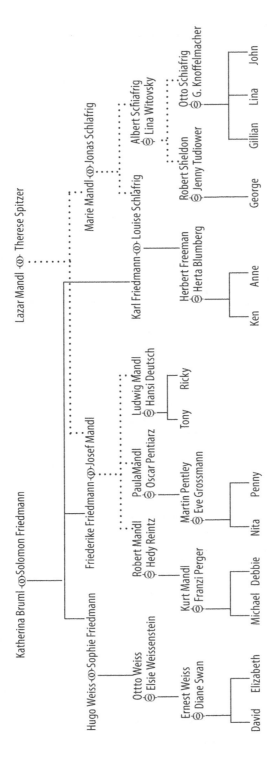

11.

COMING TO AUSTRALIA:
THE MANDLS OF NSW
AND THE SCHLAFRIGS OF WA

The Mandls of New South Wales

Most of the Mandl family in Australia arrived as refugees following the Anschluss—Nazi Germany's takeover of Austria in March 1938. Those who found a new home in Australia were extraordinarily fortunate. Thousands of European Jews sought to emigrate there. The Australian Jewish Welfare Society, organized in 1936 to assist refugees, received over 70,000 applications for assistance. By 1940, only 7,000 European Jews were able to run the gauntlet of financial and bureaucratic impediments to emigration from Central Europe to Australia. Having contacts beyond Nazi–controlled territories willing to assist made all the difference.

Like the U.S., Australia imposed quotas and demanded evidence that émigrés had means of financial support. Australia required immigrants to have "landing money" to show that they were not impecunious, and an Australian guarantor who would agree to be financially responsible for the immigrant for five years, if needed. Between 1936 and 1939, however, in response to the refugee crisis, Australia reduced the required landing money from £500 to £50 and allowed organizations to serve as guarantors. Without a guarantor, £200 landing money would suffice. Five thousand Jewish refugees arrived in 1939 alone, after which the outbreak of war virtually suspended immigration.[1]

The Mandl family's earliest contacts with Australia occurred in the 19th century with a distant relative's transgression and a missed travel connection. Emanuel "Mani" Lichtner (1854–1936) was adopted as a youngster into his cousin's large household in Moravia. As the story was told many years later:

Mani was a dynamic but badly–behaved young man, who had got a chamber maid pregnant, and so was given a one–way ticket to America. However, when he arrived in Trieste, the nearest seaport, the ship to America had sailed. Another ship was due to leave for Australia in three days' time, and he decided that this would do just as well.

Arriving in Sydney in about 1879, Mani with his entrepreneurial flair quickly fell on his feet. He went into business, entering and later taking over a successful import/export business. He managed the Austrian exhibit at the 1879 Sydney International Exhibition and later became

the Austrian consul. An elder at the main synagogue in Sydney, he married in 1887 but had no children from the marriage, and lived in a large house in Darling Point, one of Sydney's best suburbs.

Mani became friendly with the captains of ships which regularly came to Sydney and was occasionally offered a free passage to Europe when a spare cabin was available. On one visit he brought his illegitimate daughter Anna to live with him in Sydney. She was an Australian Army nurse in World War I, and later married one of her soldier patients.

Emanuel Lichtner, 1854–1936

On a visit to Vienna in the 1930s, he waxed lyrical to the assembled family about Australia as a land of opportunity, suggesting they should emigrate to escape the depressed Austrian economy. As a result [cousin] Otto Weiss, chief of the welding division of Austria's main electrical engineering company ELIN, persuaded the company to send him on a tour of its overseas agents including Australia, to investigate market opportunities.[2]

Otto Weiss spent four months in Australia in 1935, working with the ELIN representative, Charles M. Terry. Otto introduced ELIN welding equipment to industry customers all over Australia, making many invaluable contacts. Otto also got on well with Mani, then an elderly man, who wanted Otto to join him in his business. As an engineer, Otto did not see himself as a merchant, so he declined, but after returning home he regularly corresponded with Mani, always enclosing a packet of paprika, at that time not obtainable in Australia.

Otto and Else Weiss

Otto and his wife Else considered emigrating, but they deferred because of Otto's good job, the challenges of emigration, and disruption to the family and their young son Ernest's education. The Weiss's made preparations, however, and were able to leave Vienna in July 1938, not long after the Anschluss. They settled in Sydney, New South Wales, where Otto resumed his technical work from the C.M. Terry Office.

Even before Otto himself emigrated, his description of opportunities in Australia had influenced his younger first cousin, Ludwig "Lutz" Mandl, to take the plunge.

In 1937, Lutz Mandl had completed his training in electrical engineering. He was 27 years old, single, and both of his parents (Josef and Friederike Friedmann Mandl) had passed away. Economic conditions were poor and anti–Semitism on the rise in Austria. Lutz arrived in Sydney in May 1937. One of the references on his application for admission to Australia was Otto Weiss' business associate, Charles M. Terry. Lutz went right to work as an electrical engineer at the Australian Iron and Steel Works in Port Kembla, south of Sydney.

Lutz Mandl, right foreground, aboard RMS Oronsay en route to Australia, 1937

Lutz Mandl, right, in Columbo, Ceylon, en route to Australia

Lutz Mandl's immigration in 1937 ahead of the mass of Jewish refugees was fortunate for the family. Settled and employed in Australia before 1938, Lutz was able to assist his older brother Robert and sister Paula, and their families, to emigrate and to acclimate. Robert Mandl, with his wife Hedy and teenage son Kurt, and Paula Mandl with her husband Oskar Pentlarz (later Pentley) and teenage son Martin, arrived in Sydney between December 1938 and May 1939.

Not everything was smooth sailing, however. Following Australia's entry into the war in September 1939, immigrants from Germany and Austria were classified as "Enemy Aliens." As such, they were subject to a wide range of serious restrictions. Enemy Aliens were not allowed to spend the night outside their registered dwelling without permission, and not allowed to possess radios, typewriters, cameras, or automobiles. They were required to report weekly to the local police station. In addition, they were not allowed to be employed in government jobs such as radio, schools, or in any workplace connected to the military.[3]

As a single, German–speaking, military–age male émigré from Austria, Lutz Mandl was particularly subject to suspicion. When he came to the attention of security authorities, they noted that "by occupation [he] would be capable of acts of sabotage." In June 1940, Lutz lost his job at the Australian Iron and Steel Works, the company having been advised not to hire foreigners. Lutz, nonetheless, had good references and was soon employed at other firms as an electrical engineer and draftsman.

During 1940–41, despite character and loyalty endorsements from his employers and others who knew him, Lutz, because of his classification as Enemy Alien, was required to dispose of his automobile, camera, radio, and typewriter. His application to travel to visit his brother and sister in another district in June 1940 was denied. At one point in October 1940, a security official suggested that Lutz be interned along with other Enemy Aliens.

It seems strange that a Jewish refugee could be suspected of German sympathies. Although Lutz at all times identified himself as Jewish, his Austrian passport was not stamped with a large red letter "J" as were the passports of other Jewish refugees from Austria and Germany. When security authorities questioned the lack of a "J" on his passport, Lutz would explain that he left Austria in 1937, before the regulation went into effect there.[4]

Eventually of course, the investigations came to nothing. In February 1942, Lutz volunteered for the Australian army and applied for naturalization as an Australian citizen. In December 1943, he received a change in classification from Enemy Alien to Refugee Alien. Lutz became an Australian citizen in January 1945.

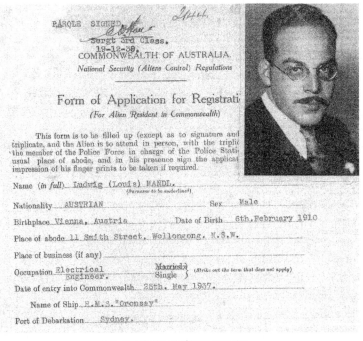

Lutz Mandl alien resident registration.

Lutz' older siblings, Robert and Paula, and their families faced obstacles in leaving Austria, but all managed to join him in Australia. In the summer of 1938, Robert Mandl arranged for a guide to walk his teenage son Kurt into Switzerland over the Alps. The guide did not show up, however, and Robert eventually found a business acquaintance to sponsor the family's entry into Britain. Robert and Kurt flew to London in September, but Hedy refused to go, and Robert had to fly back in and retrieve her. The three traveled together from London to Sydney, arriving in January 1939.

In Vienna, Robert owned a business named Gubinol Gesellschaft, which manufactured very thin gold and metal foils. Gubinol was founded in 1909 with a patent granted in 1908 to Robert's father

Josef Mandl and Richard Gubin for a machine used to prepare leaf metals for embossing. In 1938, the Nazis "aryanized" the firm, that is, confiscated it and handed it over to non–Jewish ownership.[5] In Australia, Robert turned his technical skill, business experience, and love of photography to a new enterprise—production of projection screens for photographs and films. Robert began the screen manufacturing business, Australux, in the living room of the family's apartment in Double Bay.

Gubinol foil samples booklet, 1930's..

Kurt Mandl's "Matura" from Vienna was not recognized in Australia, so in order to continue on to higher education, he was required to repeat his Matriculation Exams in New South Wales —in English of course. Kurt was successful. He then worked as a laborer at a pencil factory while studying chemical engineering at the Technical College at night. Following graduation, Kurt found work as a chemical engineer.

Before the war, Paula Mandl Pentlarz, husband Oscar, and son Martin lived in Brunn, Czechoslovakia, where Oscar was a partner in a cotton and linen weaving mill. As the situation became more alarming in the late 30's, they travelled to Prague to put Martin on a plane headed for the UK. Martin enrolled in a school in Kent where the staff had emigrated from Germany. He enjoyed his time there being taken camping in Wales, experiencing new foods, and playing the violin. His immigration permit to Australia came in late 1938. Martin travelled to Woburn House in London, headquarters of British Jewish relief organizations, to arrange a loan for his Australian landing money. On December 28, 1938, 17–year–old Martin arrived in Australia, and went to live with his uncle Lutz in Wollongong, a steel town on the south coast of New South Wales. Martin worked in a factory making metal products. He had a workplace accident and lost the tips of his two middle fingers on his left hand. Sadly, he could no longer play the violin.

One month after Oscar and Paula Pentlarz landed in Australia in May 1939, they changed the family name to Pentley. Martin went to live with his parents and help out in the "ham and beef" (delicatessen) that they operated in North Bondi, near Sydney, while he also studied engineering. It was at the shop that Martin met Eve Grossman, who he married on October 11, 1942.

Martin Pentley and Eve Grossmann Wedding Sydney, Australia, Oct. 11, 1942

The Schlafrigs of Western Australia

Another branch of the Mandl family that emigrated to Australia in the 1930s settled on the other side of the continent in Western Australia. This group descended from Marie, Lazar and Therese Mandl's first born. Marie and husband Jonas Schlafrig's six children were first cousins to Josef Mandl's three offspring Robert, Paula and Lutz Mandl. Paula's memoir, quoted above in Chapter 7, fondly recalled an early–20th century visit to her Uncle Jonas Schlafrig's home and her cousins in Mistelbach, Austria.

Albert, eldest of the Schlafrig children, became a physician like his father Jonas. In 1938, 65–year–old Albert and his wife Lina lived in Vienna as did their sons Robert, an architect, newly married to Jenny Tudiower, and Otto, a medical resident at Vienna City Hospital. Albert's sister Luise Schlafrig Friedmann was a widow with two married sons, Herbert and Victor Friedmann. Other than Victor, who emigrated to the U.S., all these Schlafrigs left Vienna during 1938–39 and found their way to Perth in Western Australia, although not travelling together as a group.

The Schlafrigs' first connection to Australia grew out of Luise Schlafrig Friedmann's vocation as a pianist and music teacher. Two young singers from Perth—Gertrude Hutton and Lorna Sydney–Smith—lived with Luise in the late 1930's while studying opera in Vienna. After the Anschluss, Lorna Sydney–Smith's father applied for Luise's son Herbert Friedmann to be admitted to Australia. Herbert and his wife Herta sailed from Rotterdam on August 31, landing in Fremantle, the port city of Perth on Oct 9, 1938.

In Vienna, Herbert had worked in the large engineering and plumbing business begun by his Friedmann grandfather and managed by his father Karl until his death in 1936. After the Nazis confiscated the business, the Friedmanns were able to leave Vienna with only their furniture (including Luise's grand piano[6]), household goods, tools of the plumbing trade, and a small amount of cash. Herbert's first employment in Perth was as a plumber. Shortly after his arrival, Herbert applied for admission to Australia for his mother Luise and for his brother Victor and wife Gerda. Victor and Gerda Friedmann, however, had managed to emigrate to New York in October 1938 assisted by an American cousin, Lester Friedmann, and decided to remain there. Luise flew from Vienna to London in March 1939 and arrived in Fremantle by ship in April.

In December 1938, Herbert's cousin Robert Schlafrig and his wife Jenny, with a reference from a firm of solicitors in Canberra, received visas for Australia from the British Consul in Vienna. Robert and Jenny departed immediately for Italy where they embarked three weeks later from Genoa to Australia via the Suez Canal and Columbo, Ceylon (Sri Lanka). They landed in Fremantle on February 8, 1939.

Meanwhile in Perth, Herbert Friedmann had met an Australian–born Jewish architect named Harold Krantz, and suggested Robert see him about opportunities there. As Krantz told the story:

[Robert] walked into my office one day and said, 'I'm an architect from Vienna and I've come to Australia as I've run away from Hitler. I'm thinking of going to Melbourne, would you advise me to go, or is there work here?'

I asked have you got any of your work you could show me, as I'm busy and I could do with some extra help.

He said, 'well, I've got a roll of plans down in the ship. I can get a taxi and bring them back to you in an hour's time. Can you see me?'

I said yes. I just opened them up, that was enough, just the glance. They were superb drawings, beautiful. Clean construction—you could see that things would work. So I said, would you like to start on Monday morning? He started and he was with me ever since, until he died [in 1968].[7]

Robert Schlafrig's Passport

Otto Schlafrig's departure from Vienna was more precipitous than that of his brother Robert. In the months following the Anschluss, the Nazi government launched a campaign of persecution and public humiliation designed to separate Jews from Austrian society. One tactic was to force Jewish men and women to publicly perform menial labor such as scrubbing the streets on hands and knees. Nazi officials encouraged children and crowds to watch and participate in these kinds of ritual humiliations, which could last hours or even days.[8] In June 1938, Otto Schlafrig was completing his three–year medical residency at the Vienna City Hospital. He was taken, nonetheless, along with other Jews to clean the streets under German guards. On the morning of June 7, the work detail's guard changed to Austrian conscripts. An Austrian guard, who happened to be a patient of Otto's father, Dr Albert Schlafrig, allowed Otto to escape. Otto and Gertrude (Trude) Knopfelmacher were married that afternoon and fled the next day to an unpoliced border crossing into Italy.

In Italy, Otto made contact with an Austrian friend living in Geneva, who helped Otto and Trude get to England. Meanwhile, through contacts in Vienna, Albert managed to bring Otto's plight to the attention of a well–known Australian physician, Dr Mary Burfitt–Williams, who sponsored Otto and Trude's entry to Australia. Nine months after leaving Vienna, Otto and Trude sailed from Genoa Italy arriving in Sydney on March 12, 1939.

Otto later joined his brother Robert in Perth and was there when their parents Albert and Lina landed in Fremantle on Oct 1, 1939. Albert and Lina had sailed from London on September 1, the day Germany invaded Poland, triggering declarations of war by Britain and France. By then, Albert's sister Luise Schlafrig Friedmann was living in Perth with her son Herbert and wife Herta Friedmann. After almost two years of struggle and uncertainty, a branch of the Schlafrig family of Vienna was safe and reunited in Western Australia.

Like Lutz Mandl in New South Wales, the Perth emigres— Herbert Friedmann, Robert and Otto Schlafrig—encountered some roadblocks to acceptance in Australia. First was the problem of being young, male "Enemy Aliens" while the country was at war. Second was Australian resistance to non–British immigrants, especially those seen as competition in the professional and labor force. While many Australians were welcoming and helpful, some were not; a measure of antisemitism may have been involved as well.

Herbert Friedman and Robert Schlafrig, like Lutz Mandl, experienced directly the problem of "Enemy Alien" status. As anti–

German feelings intensified in Australia with the fall of Belgium and the Netherlands in June 1940, forty–nine German–speaking refugees and emigres in Western Australia, including Robert and Herbert, were arrested and interned in the Fremantle Prison. Most, including Robert and Herbert, were released after three weeks, the authorities having determined that they were no threat to national security.[9] The experience, however, must have been jarring, perhaps especially to Herbert who was supporting his mother and pregnant wife.[10] Both Herbert and Herta wrote to the security authorities arguing for his release. Herbert referred to his internment as a "terrible shock," and Herta noted that Herbert had been among the first to offer his services to the Australian military forces should a Foreign Legion of Jewish emigres be formed to fight the Nazis. Herbert's employer, as well as the architect Harold Krantz, Mr. Sydney Smith, and several other neighbors and friends also wrote attesting to his character and loyalty.[11]

Release from internment did not end the security authorities' scrutiny. In 1941–42, Herbert suffered the same sorts of restrictions as Lutz Mandl had experienced—limitations on travel, ownership and use of a car and a camera. With respect to entering trades and professions, both Herbert Friedmann and Otto Schlafrig faced barriers early on. Although Herbert was employed almost immediately after arrival in Perth by a plumbing company, both the plumbers' union and the Returned Soldiers League, an association of WWI veterans, objected to his employment as a plumber and to his membership in the union, ostensibly because he was an alien. The plumbing company nevertheless retained Herbert, but more in a sales and administrative capacity, at least until 1942 when his presence threatened the company's government contracts. Like Lutz, Herbert was forced to leave his job because his employer had contracts for work on military installations. He became the manager of a sheet metal factory, where he remained for the rest of his working life.

For the medical profession, the status of refugee doctors became a pressing political issue in Australia in the years 1938–43. Generally, a degree from a British or Australian medical school was required for admission to practice medicine. Some Australian doctors and medical officials feared an "influx of German Jewish refugee practitioners" and resisted allowing them into the profession. The outbreak of war in September 1939 changed the situation as medical personnel left their positions and enlisted in the armed services. The shortage of medical expertise eventually led to a relaxation of barriers to refugee doctors' practice.

Otto Schlafrig's story is related in an Australian journal of medical history:

Like many other refugees, Otto Schlafrig worked selling Watkins Products door-to-door. ... On his detailing rounds he had become acquainted with a Miss Ottaway, who was either employed by or knew the Minister for Health. She alerted the minister to the plight of foreign doctors and of Schlafrig in particular. As a consequence, the legislation on alien registration was eventually changed and Schlafrig sat and passed the examination of the Commonwealth Alien Doctors Board.

Even then, and despite his comprehensive previous experience in Vienna, Otto was required to spend part of 1941 at Perth Hospital as a resident, proving his competency.[12]

After 1942, the family's efforts to assimilate proceeded more smoothly. In 1942, Otto became a general practitioner in Kondinin, a small rural town 160 miles east of Perth. Robert Schlafrig enlisted in the Citizen Military Force, a part–time reserve of the Australian Military Force, where he served as a "sapper" (engineer) from 1942–44. In 1944, Robert and Jenny were naturalized as Australian citizens. In October 1943, all of the Friedmanns were granted "Refugee Alien" status. They became Australian citizens and changed their name from Friedmann to Freeman.

By the end of 1944, Albert Schlafrig, a widower since Lina's death in 1941, was living on a poultry farm in Stoneville, a suburb of Perth. (Albert undoubtedly recalled the chickens raised at his childhood home in Mistelbach, also mentioned in his cousin Paula Mandl Pentley's memoir, quoted in Chapter 7 of this book.) Albert was partners in Stoneville with Kate Rosendorff, a 1939 German emigre widowed in 1941. On Dec. 31 and Jan. 2, 1944–45, Albert wrote to his sister Clara and brother-in-law David Mandl, who had been living in New York since 1940:

Thank you for your birthday wishes. I passed my birthday (the 71st! How time flies) here in Stoneville and took the highest pleasure in the fact that [sister] Luise [Schlafrig Friedmann] was our visitor here at this time for about 10 days. [Luise lived in Perth with son Herbert and his wife Herta.] She liked her stay here and recovered after all the hard work she has to do and we really enjoyed her company. It is true somebody said she felt everywhere better than at home and it is fact indeed that she cannot agree with Herta and does not like her ways, but I think she really likes the peace & quiet and nice and clean and comfortable as it is here and she has promised to come and to keep company to Mrs Rosendorff during the time when I will go to Otto to see him and his family. ...

Little Georgie [George Schlafrig/Sheldon, age 2 1/2] got whooping cough. He is not too bad but I am sorry for the little chap. Bobby is quite upset and can't enjoy his Xmas leave. ...

2/1/45 Otto rang me up just now to inform me that he became father of another daughter [Gillian] this morning. Everything allright. They are very happy although Trude will have to work hard to keep the house clean. It is very difficult to get any help especially in the country. ... Otto rather busy. People like him and the neighbouring towns (14 and 32 miles distant) are deliberating about paying him his expenses if he would come once a week for consulting hours as it is not easy for patients there to come to his consultation in Kondinin in consequence of petrol restriction.

As for me, I am living very quietly and happy here in Stoneville. I have no responsibilities, little worries and I don't think that I should be happier if I was registered [to practice medicine] and had to work again in my profession in some remote place.

Drs. Otto and Albert Schlafrig

Post–War Lives—Western Australia

When Kate Rosendorff died in 1957 at age 68, Albert Schlafrig was 84 years old. In 1958, Albert took a solo trip around the world. He went first to Europe where he likely visited with the few friends and family still living in Vienna—including brother Gustav Schlafrig's widow Josefa and daughter Helga—and took a cruise in Norway. In September, Albert sailed from London to New York on the Queen Elizabeth. In the U.S., Albert could see his sister Clara Schlafrig Mandl, and several of the next two generations of Mandl and Schlafrig nieces, nephews, and cousins, some of whom he knew in Vienna and some he had not yet met. Otto Mandl (see Chapter 10) recalled "Uncle Albert" making a house call when he was a small child in Vienna and then his visit in New York so many years later. Otto recalled particularly how his own young children were fascinated by Albert's great white beard and charmed by his gentle manner and little carved wood animals he brought for them—kangaroos, perhaps.

In California, Albert visited with Gerda Strauss Friedmann/ Freeman, his nephew Victor's widow, and their daughter Mary Louise Freeman (Jaffray), then 12 years old. Mary Louise also recalled Albert's "wonderful white hair and very bushy white beard." She said that her mother seemed quite fond of him, and "he did leave with me the feeling and impression of a very warm, interested, and interesting person along with a bracelet that I treasured for many years (unfortunately stolen in a burglary in 1995)." Albert sailed home from San Francisco with stops in Honolulu and Sydney, arriving in Fremantle on November 26, 1958. He passed away in 1966 at age 93.

After the war, Albert's sons thrived in their professions. In 1946, Robert and Jenny Schlafrig changed their last name to Sheldon, at which time the architectural firm of Krantz and Sheldon was formed. The Sheldons' only child, George, became an architect and a partner in the firm in 1965, just three years before his father died. Otto Schlafrig relocated in 1953 from Kondinin to Perth where he purchased a medical practice. He and Trude raised three children— Lina, John, and Gillian who became a fourth–generation physician.

Luise Schlafrig Friedmann/Freeman continued to live with her son Herbert, daughter–in–law Herta, and their two children Kenneth

Charles and Anne until she moved into a care home a few years before she died in 1964. The relationship between Luise and Herta did not improve, which is probably unsurprising given that they were both strong–willed, accomplished women. Luise, for example, was a serious pianist and teacher whose connections with the professional music world in Vienna had created the family's contacts with Australia.

Luise Schlafrig Friedmann/Freeman

Herta and Herbert Friedmann/Freeman, Anne Freeman
Greville, 1968

Herta had a law degree from the University of Vienna but was not able to practice law in Australia. She was also a physiotherapist, which she practiced as a part time job.

Herbert Freeman managed the sheet metal factory until retirement, after which he returned to his longstanding interest in classics, obtaining a university degree in Greek and Latin and eventually a PhD at the age of 77. Herta passed away in 1969. In 1974 Herbert married Zena Webster, an ophthalmologist twenty years his junior, to whom he was happily married until he passed away in 1981.

Post–War Lives—New South Wales

In 1946, after seven years of war–censored correspondence, Kurt Mandl married his pre–war teenage sweetheart, Franziska (Franzi) Perger. Franzi had emigrated from Vienna to England with her parents, and then to the U.S. in 1944. She arrived in Australia on May 27, 1946, and married Kurt three weeks later.

l to r: Lutz Mandl, unknown lady, Franzi, Kurt, Hedy (Hedwig) Reinitz Mandl and Robert Mandl
Wedding of Kurt Mandl and Franzi Perger, Temple Emanuel, Woollahra, NSW, Australia, June 16, 1946,

In 1949, Kurt's father Robert died suddenly from a heart attack, and Kurt was thrown into control of Australux, the projection screen company Robert had founded in Australia. Kurt, working with Franzi and his mother Hedy, built up Australux into a manufacturer and supplier of projection screens throughout Australia. Using his chemical engineering knowledge, Kurt developed several methods to further improve the quality of the product.

Kurt Mandl was a person of broad interests. Befitting young men raised in Austria, Kurt, his uncle Lutz Mandl, and cousin Martin Pentley were all skiing enthusiasts who enjoyed introducing the next generations to the sport. Kurt and Franzi also participated as actors in the Viennese Theatre in Sydney. On retirement, Kurt studied drawing and French, and took part in several community organizations such as the Scouts, which his children Michael and Debbie had joined.

Kurt's aunt Paula Mandl Pentley was very much a woman of her times—a talented member of an accomplished Viennese family who was stymied by her gender and by the political and social upheavals that affected her generation. Paula loved literature and music, and like so many in the family, played the piano. She had ambitions as a writer and in Australia produced a set of memoirs in English—like the one quoted in Chapter 7—that eloquently describe her world. With regard to her teenage years during the First World War, for example, she wrote:

Though success was not with me in the question of my studying medicine, my father—alarmed by the distress his refusal had caused me—didn't place too many difficulties in my way when I declared that I wanted to help with the communal soup kitchens the war years in Vienna had made such urgent necessity. Not only did the stream of fugitives from the advancing Russian Army converge in Vienna but the general impoverishment of the middle class and the difficulties in obtaining sufficient food drove people who in days past would have turned up their noses at any but first class restaurants to these eating places.

Coming to Australia as a refugee herself, Paula was in no better position to pursue her ambitions. After she and Oscar sold the ham and beef shop, Oscar worked as a bookkeeper and Paula had various jobs—office work in a hospital, typing for a doctor, and finally as secretary and assistant to Kurt Offenburg, a German journalist and intellectual who had become a respected political commentator and radio broadcaster in Australia.

Paula's son Martin recalled that Paula was energized by working for Offenburg and greatly valued him and his work. Offenburg was an internationalist committed to promoting world peace. When Offenburg died unexpectedly in 1946 at age 47, Paula became the Honorary Secretary and driving force of a Memorial Fund, which in 1950 created the Kurt Offenburg Memorial Collection at the State Library of Victoria, begun with Offenburg's collection of over 400 books focused on international affairs and world understanding. After speaking at the Collection's dedication, Paula wrote to the Chief Librarian:

I know it is only a small thing at present, compared with other big collections, but I am not ashamed to say that I have faith in its future and that it will one day honor its dedication. I am not foolish enough to think it might prevent war and disaster, but if it only achieves to make people think a bit more broadmindedly and at the same time objectively it will mean a step further.

Paula Mandl Pentley ca. 1948

Following Paula's death in 1957, Oscar Pentley wrote: "Knowing and understanding how deep in the heart of my late wife was the desire to perpetuate Mr. Offenburg's work, I was contemplating in which way I could continue her work." From then on—in fact, until 1972 —a cheque for 15 guineas was sent each year to the Library Trustees, "to be applied by them in the purchase of suitable books to be added to the Kurt Offenburg Memorial Collection at the Library and to be inscribed 'In Memory of Paula Pentley.'"[13]

After studying mechanical engineering and working a few years as a draftsman, Martin Pentley joined his in–laws' leather wholesale and retail firm, where he continued until retirement. Leather House Grossman was a successful business that supported several families. Martin traveled widely for the firm, conducting business in Europe and Asia, and took charge of the firm when his father–in–law died in 1965. Like his uncle Lutz and cousin Kurt, Martin was a cross country skier, as well as an ardent bushwalker. He trekked to base camp Mt. Everest with a group of hikers led by Paddy Pallin, Australia's pioneering outdoorsman. Martin passed on his love of the outdoors to his and Eve's two daughters, Nita Kent and Penny Pentley, and to his grandchildren.

In 1980, Martin Pentley converted to Catholicism, as had Eve years before. He was an enthusiastic participant in his Church. In a heartfelt eulogy in the Church newsletter when Martin died in 2010, the parish priest wrote, "In terms of many ministries in the parish, we will have to re–structure, re–imagine, and re–commit ourselves to the roles that Martin has filled so well for so long."

Martin Pentley and daughter Nita Pentley Kent, May 1971

In 1946, Lutz Mandl met Hansi Deutsch, also a 1938 emigre from Vienna, at a dance at the Austria Society in Sydney. They married on October 19, 1946 at Temple Emanuel Synagogue in Sydney.

Using the technical training and business acumen he acquired working for others during the war years, Lutz formed his own company importing component parts and industrial testing equipment from Asia and Europe, affording him the opportunity

Ludwig and Hansi Deutsch Mandl,
Temple Emanuel, Sydney, Australia, 1946

for international travel. Just as Lutz was the forward–thinking adventurous one who, in 1937, came out to Australia alone in advance of the rest of the family, he continued to be ahead of his times—an amateur inventor of forward–looking products, mostly a vegetarian, and a Tai Chi practitioner. Like his nephews Kurt Mandl and Martin Pentley, Lutz was an outdoorsman—skiing in the Snowy Mountains, swimming weekly in ocean pools or in the bay. Lutz introduced his son Tony and daughter Ricky to these sports, as well as to classical music, taking up piano himself in retirement.

Ricky Mandl Davis with parents
Hansi and Lutz Mandl, Sydney, Australia, 1980

During the second half of the twentieth century, the Mandls in eastern Australia and Schlafrigs in the west built new lives and prospered. Their Australian–born children obtained good educations, good jobs, married, and had children of their own. What they did not do—understandably given their busy lives and the limitations of distance—was stay in close touch with each other.

The benefits of electronic communications in the 21ˢᵗ century, however, made it possible for the families to re–connect, not only with their Australian cousins but internationally. In 2009, Ricky Mandl Davis, daughter of Lutz Mandl, flew from Sydney to Perth where she met for the first time her cousins Gillian Schlafrig, daughter of Otto Schlafrig, and Anne Freeman Greville, daughter of Herbert Freeman.

In May 2014, Ricky and Anne traveled from Australia to New York. At the Museum of Jewish Heritage overlooking the Statue of Liberty in New York harbor, Ricky and Anne met June Friedman Entman, great–granddaughter of Jacob Mandl.

Ricky Mandl Davis, June Friedman Entman, Anne Freeman
Greville, NY, 2014. Photo credit: Michael Davis

Arthur Frotten, June Entman, John Schlafrig,
St. Augustine, FL, Dec. 31, 2019
Photo credit: Howard Entman

In 2019, Floridian Art Frotten, grandson of Friedrich Schlafrig, and Australian John Schlafrig, grandson of Albert Schlafrig, along with their spouses, celebrated New Year's Eve at their cousin June Entman's home in St. Augustine, Florida.

These were, by far, not the only Mandl family cousins to meet or gatherings to take place; these reunions, active correspondences, and sharing of family lore are continuing well into the 21st century.

Notes

1 *The Australian People: An Encyclopedia of the Nation, Its People, and Their Origins*, ed. James Jupp, Center for Immigration and Multicultural Studies, Australian National University (1988) p. 534; *Safe Haven: Records of the Jewish Experience in Australia*, National Archives of Australia, 1999.

2 Ernest and Ken Weiss, *How Lucky We Were*, in Erinnerungen/Lives Remembered, vol. 5, pp. 196–98, The National Fund of the Republic of Austria for Victims of National Socialism, 2018.

3 *Safe Haven: Records of the Jewish Experience in Australia*, National Archives of Australia 1999, p. 74.

4 The Nazi government required Jews to identify themselves in ways that would permanently separate them from the rest of the German population. In October 1938, the government invalidated all German (including Austrian) passports held by Jews. Jews were required to surrender their old passports, which became valid only after the letter "J" was stamped on them. https://www.ushmm.org/learn/timeline-ofevents/1933–1938/reich–ministry–of–the–interior–invalidates–all–german–passports–held–by–jew.

5 After the war, Robert reached a settlement with the manager to whom the Nazi government had given the company. Gubinol remains in existence in Vienna.

6 Jews emigrating from Austria who could afford to do so had household goods delivered to freight forwarders for export. For a time after the Anschluss, these shipments continued. Otto and Else Weiss' furniture shipment, for example, arrived in Sydney about a month after they did in September 1938. Eventually, the shipments were stopped and seized by the Nazi government. https://www.kunstdatenbank.at/the–vugesta–the–gestapo–office–for–the–disposal–of–the–property–of–jewishemigrants.

7 www.thekrantzlegacy.com/robert–sheldon.

8 Ilana Fritz Offenberger, *The Jews of Nazi Vienna*, 1938–1945, pp. 41–47 (2017).

9 Sally Quin, *Bauhaus on the Swan*, p. 67 (2015); Mary Mennicken, *The Germans in Western Australia : Innovators, Immigrants, Internees* (1993).

10 Kenneth Charles Freeman, Duffield Professor Emeritus, Research School of Astronomy & Astrophysics, The Australian National University, 2012 recipient of the Prime Minister's Prize for Science, was born to the Friedmanns on August 27, 1940.

11 National Archives of Australia: PP302/1, WA14772.

12 Peter Winterton, Alien Doctors: The Western Australian Medical Fraternity's Reaction to European Events 1930–50, 7 *Health and History* pp. 71–81 (2005).

13 Walter Struve, "Dedicated to the Promotion of International Understanding": A Memorial for Kurt Offenburg at the State Library, 78 *The La Trobe Journal*, Spring *2006*.

12.

SURVIVING THE HOLOCAUST
IN AUSTRIA AND HUNGARY

Not all our family members were able to escape the Holocaust in Europe. The Nazis murdered some, some died of deprivation and disease in concentration camps, some disappeared. Their names and photos, if we have them, appear in the next chapter.

A handful of our relatives survived the Holocaust in Europe through courage, strength, determination, luck, and assistance from other brave souls both Jewish and non–Jewish:

Friedrich and Fanny Schlaefrig were deported from Vienna and survived three years in the Theresienstadt concentration camp.

Friedrich's brother Gustav Schlafrig lost his career due to his Jewish birth but avoided deportation because of his Catholic marriage.

Zsuzsanna Frank, Bernhard Mandl's granddaughter, was deported from Budapest to Dachau, from which she escaped towards the end of the war.

Paul Sondhoff, son of Louis Goldberger's first cousin Helene Goldberger Sondhoff, hid in an attic in Vienna for four years.

Julius Dutka, former husband of Klara Mandl, and Olga Blumberg, mother of Herta Freeman, were two of the 982 refugees who were allowed into the U.S. as "guests" of President Franklin D. Roosevelt and housed at Fort Ontario in Oswego, New York from August 1944 until February 1946.

The Brothers Schlafrig in Vienna

In the 1930's, two of the Mistelbach Schlafrigs, Friedrich and Gustav, were successful architects, married and raising children in Vienna. (See Chapter 7.) Gustav Schlafrig (1881–1950) and his wife Josepha Kammellander had a daughter, Helga. Friedrich (1875–1953) and his wife Fanny Witovsky (1886–1965) had two children — Wilhelm and Marie.

In 1938, Friedrich "Fritz" Schlafrig was 64 and retired from his career as an architectural engineer and official in the Austrian Railroad Ministry. He was active as president of the largest B'nai B'rith Lodge in Vienna. Fritz and Fanny's son Wilhelm "Willy" had completed his university degree and moved to South Africa in 1936, where he began his architecture career. Their daughter, 27–year–old Marie, had studied art and design. Having found a position in London as a domestic servant and nanny, however, she escaped Vienna around New Year's 1939. Marie married a Canadian soldier in England in 1943 and became Mary Frotten.

Marie Schlafrig Frotten—Exempt from Internment in England

On several occasions between 1938 and 1942, Fritz was arrested and released by the Gestapo. He and Fanny were deprived of most of their possessions and forced to move repeatedly into smaller and more crowded quarters. Attempts by Willy in South Africa and relatives in Australia and the U.S. to obtain visas and travel permits for Fritz and Fanny were all unsuccessful.[1] In September 1942, the Schlafrigs were transported to the ghetto/concentration camp at Theresienstadt (Terezin), Czechoslovakia.

Theresienstadt was a town used by Nazi Germany from 1941 to 1945 as a walled ghetto, or concentration camp, and as a transit camp for Jews en route to Auschwitz and other extermination camps. The Nazis intended the camp to house elderly, privileged, and famous Jews, and allowed the inmates to administer the severely overcrowded camp on a day to day basis. As the home—and the place of death—of some of the most prominent Czech, Austrian, and German artists, writers, scientists, jurists, diplomats, musicians, and scholars, Theresienstadt had a rich cultural life including schools, theaters and orchestras. In 1943, to dispel rumors about the extermination camps, the Nazis permitted a Red Cross delegation to visit Theresienstadt, where they had arranged an elaborate hoax. They deported many camp residents to Auschwitz to minimize the crowding and erected fake residences, stores, and cafés to give the appearance of a comfortable life. A children's opera was performed for the guests. The hoax succeeded so well that the Nazis made a propaganda film at Theresienstadt showing how well the Jews were living under their benevolent protection. Nonetheless, of the approximately 144,000 Jews sent to Theresienstadt, some 33,000—almost 1 in 4—died there from malnutrition and disease, and about 88,000 were deported to Auschwitz and other death camps. By the war's end, only 19,000 were alive.

Fritz and Fanny survived three years in Theresienstadt. In August of 1946, they were residing in a Red Cross Displaced Persons facility in Paris awaiting arrangements to join their son Willy (now William Shaw) in South Africa. Daughter Mary Frotten had moved with her husband to Canada in August 1945, afterwards settling in Detroit, Michigan.

While in Paris, Fritz and Fanny met David Boder, a professor of psychology at the Illinois Institute of Technology who had traveled to Europe for the purpose of interviewing displaced persons throughout the continent. Over several months, Boder conducted and recorded 130 interviews, more than ninety hours, on two hundred magnetic wire spools.[2] Boder interviewed Fritz Schlafrig at the Paris offices of the American Jewish Joint Distribution Committee. The hour and twenty–minute interview is preserved, transcribed, translated into English, and available to hear and read at https://voices.library.iit.edu/interview/schlaefrigF.

In the interview, Fritz describes life under the Nazis in Vienna before deportation and the hellish conditions in Theresienstadt, where Fritz tried to use his engineering skills to improve conditions and Fanny worked at times as a nurse and in a mica production workshop. Toward the end of 1944, the couple's strength was so depleted that they survived only because of the occasional food packages received via the Red Cross sent from relatives, including Gustav.

Even more remarkably, Dr. Boder was able to keep a promise to the Schlafrigs to contact their daughter when he returned to the U.S. Mary Frotten never saw her father again, but she did hear his voice in September 1947 when Boder, attending a meeting of the American Psychological Association in Detroit, played the recorded interview for her.

Hearing Parents' Voices From DP Camp

Mrs. Mary Frotten, 2141 Antoinette street, had a unique experience at the convention of the American Psychological Association. She heard, via the magnetic wire recorder, her parents' voices addressed to her from a displaced persons' camp in Europe. She had not heard their voices for nine years. With her as she listens is Dr. David P. Boder, of Chicago.
—News Photo.

* * *   * * *

Recorder Stirs Memories   6—THE DETROIT NEWS
                              SATURDAY, SEPTEMBER 13, 1947
of a Family Split by War

The Detroit News, Detroit, Michigan, September 13, 1947

Another astonishing artifact from Theresienstadt is a 148–page handwritten recipe book that the Schlafrigs produced there. Commercially–produced cookbooks were not common in those days. Most women, when they became homemakers, kept their own notebooks of recipes handed down and exchanged from family and friends. It was a common tradition for daughters to inherit a book of handwritten recipes from their mothers. Those incarcerated in Theresienstadt must have assumed that their personal books were lost to them, and at the same time, the internees were obsessed with food, which was in desperately short supply. Discussing food and recreating recipe books from memory, on whatever sorts of paper available, was a means of remembering good times and imagining a better future. Several similar manuscripts have survived.[3]

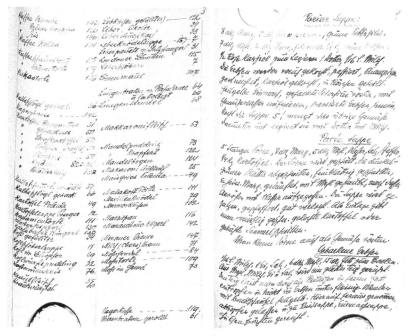

Schlafrigs' Theresienstadt Recipe Book, contents and recipe page

Fanny was able to pass along the Theresienstadt recipe book—several hundred recipes written on the thin pages of a ledger–type book, complete with alphabetized index—to her daughter Mary Frotten when Fanny traveled to Detroit on a visit from South Africa in

1960. After Mary's death in 2011, her son Arthur Frotten donated the book and other Schlafrig documents to the U.S. Holocaust Memorial Museum in Washington D.C.[4]

Arthur Frotten with his Schlafrig grandparents'
Theresienstadt recipe book, 2015

In South Africa, William Shaw followed not only his father's career in architecture, but also his interest in classical music and violin construction. Willy and his wife Hilda Shaw raised two children —Arthur Leslie Shaw, a third generation architect, and Sheila von Heynitz, a fashion designer like her aunt Mary. In 1969, Mary Frotten and her son Arthur visited the Shaws in South Africa. By then, both Fritz and Fanny had passed away.

Friedrich's younger brother Gustav Schläfrig was most probably the only Jewish architect who remained in Vienna during the Nazi era and survived.[5] Gustav converted to Catholicism when he married Josepha in 1922. Daughter Helga, born in 1925, was baptized and raised Catholic. After the Anschluss, Gustav Schläfrig's license to practice his profession was revoked due to his Jewish origins. His "mixed marriage," however, saved him from deportation. Living half underground and working secretly for other construction offices, Gustav was able to send food parcels to relatives who had been deported to Theresienstadt, which enabled them to survive. After the war, Gustav regained his license and worked for a few years as a self–employed architect until his death in 1950.[6] Gustav's daughter Helga Schlafrig was a Ph. D. professor of music and for over 50 years the principal organist at St. Ulrich, the second largest church in Vienna. She was devoted to teaching young musicians and to the preservation of St. Ulrich, with which she was closely connected her entire life. Helga passed away in 2020 in Vienna at age 95.

John Schlafrig, son of Otto Schlafrig, visiting from Australia
with Helga Schlafrig at her home in Vienna 2016.

Zsuzsa Turi's Escape to the Forest

When war came to Hungary in 1939, 15–year–old Zsuzsanna (Zsuzsa) Frank lived, as she had her whole life, with her parents, uncle, and grandparents in Budapest. Grandfather was the eldest Mandl son, Bernhard—scholar, principal of the first Jewish secondary school in Hungary, family genealogist. Zsuzsa's mother and grandmother were also teachers; her father and uncle were civil servants.

At age 88 in 1940, Bernhard Mandl passed away. Paula Mandl Pentley, in Australia after the war, wrote about Bernhard, "My aged uncle, teacher and scholar, whom I loved for his profound wisdom and knowledge, had the good fortune to die shortly before the war—all of us with aged parents in Europe had come to regard it as a thing of luck if our dear ones had gone to rest before the advent of Hitler."

Zsuzsanna Frank, ca.1937

Hungary was initially allied with Nazi Germany in World War II. Nonetheless, in March 1944 Germany invaded and occupied Hungary because the Nazis feared that Hungary was in peace negotiations with the U.S. and U. K. Until then, some Hungarian Jews had been sent to labor camps, and Jews were restricted from professions, businesses, and public life, but mass deportations to killing centers began only in 1944. By then, Zsuzsa's father Arnold Frank, her uncle Raphael Mandl, and her fiancé Istvan (Stephan) Turi had all been sent to labor camps.

In November 1944 Zsuzsa was arrested and deported to Dachau. She survived typhus, starvation, and brutal treatment until, as the war was ending in May 1945, she and a camp friend escaped. They overheard a German officer saying that the "Haftlings" (slaves) were to be murdered, so they slipped away into the surrounding forest when the electricity to the camp was off and the electric fences disarmed. Zsuzsa was hiding in the woods when, unbeknownst to her, the war ended. Also unknown to both her and her cousin Charlie Winter was that he was only about 15 miles away with the U.S. Army moving across Germany. The next stop for Zsuzsa was a refugee camp in Germany and eventual return to Budapest.[7]

In a letter to her cousin Paula Mandl Pentley in Australia, Zsuzsa's mother, Sara Frank, thanked Paula for parcels she had sent, and related the family's post–war ordeals. Paula included Sara's descriptions in an essay:

After the Russians had liberated Budapest [in February 1945], the two older women [Sara and Bernhard's widow, Ester] returned to their empty house that in the course of war had been bombed, so that only two rooms had a roof. With odd bits of furniture they managed to get hold of, they started the semblance of a home. No warm clothes in the bitterly cold European winter, hardly anything to eat and no money at all.... [S]ome time later Sarah's daughter [Zsuzsa] returned from the camp, sick, exhausted, but alive and back. And as, again after some time, even her husband [Arnold] returned, they felt that, in spite of their terrible experiences and impaired health, they had been rather fortunate. A few days after her husband had started a job, a brick from a bomb–shattered house struck him on the head and he died after an unsuccessful operation, leaving the three women to face the insecurity, want and racial enmity of a war-ravaged city alone.

Zsuzsa was also greeted at home by other losses. Her uncle Raphael did not return, killed, most likely, in 1943. Her fiancée Istvan's entire family, including his parents, had been killed in Budapest. Istvan himself had lost both of his feet from frostbite in the labor camp.

Zsuzsa and Istvan married and completed their education—Istvan as an attorney, Zsuzsa earning a Ph. D. in Physics. Istvan became a prosecutor, judge, and law professor. Their only child, a son Andras, became an attorney, prosecutor, and teacher as well. Zsuzsa had an illustrious career, especially for a woman in those days, at the Hungarian Central Research Institute of Physics. She was Editor of the Hungarian Journal of Physics for over 50 years, and for 40 years,

she served as Deputy Secretary Generale of the Federation of Technical and Scientific Societies of Hungary.

Zsuzsa stayed in touch with her cousins and childhood playmates Charlie and Marianne Winter in the U.S. (See Chapter 7.) Charlie Winter saw Zsuzsa briefly in 1985 on a visit to East Berlin. In 1988, Istvan needed hip replacements

Zsuzsa Frank Turi, at home in Budapest SHOAH testimony 2001

Zsuzsa Frank Turi with
Anita Boggia Mandl, Budapest, 2010

after botched surgeries in Budapest. Zsuzsa wanted to arrange for surgery for him in Vienna, but living behind the Iron Curtain, she had no hard currency to take out of Hungary. Charlie helped his sister Marianne, who was herself terminally ill at the time, send $10,000 to Zsuzsa for the hospital in Vienna. The Viennese doctor performed the successful surgery without seeking payment.

Paul Sondhoff: Hidden in Vienna

Agnes and Paul Sondhoff, Vienna, ca. 1936

Paul and Alma Agnes Sondhoff, born in 1923 and 1930 in Vienna, were the children of Alfons Sondhoff, an engineer, and Helene Goldberger Sondhoff. Helene was a first cousin of Louis J. Goldberger of Brooklyn, New York. Lou's import business brought him to Austria numerous times during the 1920's, so it is likely that he met his uncle Joseph Goldberger's family, including the Sondhoffs and young Paul.[8]

In 1938, after Jewish children were expelled from Viennese public schools, Paul was one of the fortunate few admitted to Chajes Gymnasium, a Jewish secondary school. As a classmate later described the situation, "Access was limited to Jewish honor students selected from all the schools in Vienna…. It was the most extraordinary school, the most extraordinary class and the most extraordinary atmosphere. Can you imagine the very best 15–year–old Jewish students of Vienna in one classroom!... The official curriculum was thrown out of the window and we pushed ahead up to and beyond university level." The school remained open only until the end of the 1939 school year, with students frequently disappearing as their families were able to emigrate. Nonetheless, some lifelong friendships were forged during that short time.

Students at Chajes Gymnasium in Vienna during the school year 1938/39

In the above photo, Paul Sondhoff is on the top row, center. To his left, Walter Kohn, who sixty years later won the Nobel Prize in Chemistry. To Walter's left is Herbert Neuhaus, who became a physician in Illinois. Several other classmates became professors of mathematics, including Rodolfo Permutti at the University of Trieste, and Gertrude Ehrlich, bottom right, at the University of Maryland. Gertrude later wrote, "One day, our classmate Bibi [Paul] entertained us with music: he had discovered a way to play tunes on his fountain pen.... The class got smaller and smaller as the year progressed—the lucky ones got their visa early. Emigration was on everyone's mind."[9]

Paul's family did not manage to emigrate. His parents, Alfons and Helene, had been separated for several years.[10] On Sept. 1, 1940, Alfons died unexpectedly of a heart attack.[11] Thereafter, in exchange for assurances that his mother and sister would be safe from deportation, Paul volunteered for a labor detail at Traunkirchen in Upper Austria.

Over 400 Viennese Jews did construction work on roads and tunnels under brutal conditions at a camp called Arbeitslager Traunsee. Most, including some like Paul who were first sent back to Vienna, were subsequently sent to killing centers. By one count, only 17 of the group survived the war as "u–boats," i.e. in hiding, in Vienna.[12]

While Paul was away, Alfons' sister Anny[13] came to Vienna from Moravia to assist the family. Because Anny was never registered as residing in the city, and moved around frequently staying with different friends, she was in less danger of deportation than Helene and Agnes. Anny was able to protect them and herself for some time by bribing an SS official, but she was ultimately betrayed. In June 1942, shortly after Paul had returned to Vienna from over a year at Traunsee, Helene and Agnes were deported. They were killed upon their arrival at Maly Trostinec, but Paul and Anny did not know their fate until after the war.

Anny found a hiding place for Paul in the attic of his former Latin teacher, Frau Professor Mattha.[14] Paul was able to leave the small attic room only when the Professor's aunt, who lived there as well and could not be trusted, was out of the apartment. Until the war's end, Anny's life was harrowing, moving around the city, eking out an existence for herself and Paul.[15] Anny and Paul were two of the 600 or so "u–boats" who surfaced in Vienna after the liberation in 1945.[16]

After the war, Paul completed his education at the Technical University in Vienna before coming to the U.S. in 1951, where he lived at first in Brooklyn with his mother's cousins, Louis and Nellie Goldberger. On September 7, 1952, Nellie wrote to her daughter Eleanor, "Paul walked in yesterday with a bouquet of flowers as today is the day he arrived a year ago.... Paul is looking for a furnished

Paul Sondhoff, Brooklyn, NY, 1951

apt. to share with a friend. Pop is discouraging him. He's afraid he might get into mischief and Pop's responsible for him."

Paul worked at the Kearfott Company in New Jersey where he was Engineering Manager for the gyros used on the controversial Skybolt ballistic missile in 1962. He married Cristel (Christine) Gaiser in 1961. They lived in Upper Montclair, N.J. until his death in 1993. After Paul's death, Cristel returned to Bavaria where her two sons from a previous marriage lived with their families. She died in January 2008 in Laufen, Germany. Paul's name is engraved on her tombstone in Salzach.

Paul and Cristel Sondhoff wedding day, 1961
L–r behind seated Cristel and Paul: Ottilie Winter, Eleanor Goldberger Friedman, Lou and Nellie Goldberger, Fritz Winter. (Ottilie, daughter of David and Clara Mandl, came to the US with husband Fritz in September, 1939. They are parents of Charlie and Marianne Winter. See Chapter 10.)

Anny married Massimo (Max) Ceiger[17] in 1962 and continued living in Vienna until her death in 1995. Paul and Anny visited each other over the years in both Vienna and the U.S In the summer of 1964, Paul and Anny had plans to fly from New Jersey to Atlanta to see Lou and Nellie Goldberger who had moved there to be near their daughter Eleanor. Nellie died unexpectedly, however, on July 8, and they attended her funeral in New York instead.[18]

Paul's Bear

The Holocaust Exhibition at the Imperial War Museum in London opened in the year 2000. The exhibit included a glass case displaying a tattered mechanical toy bear identified as belonging to Paul Sondhoff, who was hidden in Vienna between 1941 and 1945.

Paul Sondhoff's bear was on loan to the Holocaust Exhibition from the family of Walter and Rachel Ginsburg Foster. Walter J. Foster (formerly Fast) (1923–2009) was another of Paul's new-found friends at Chajes Gymnasium. Walter left Vienna on a Kindertransport in 1939 and returned to Vienna in 1945 as a soldier in the British army.[19] When Walter scanned the lists of survivors looking for anyone he had known before the war, he

Paul Sondhoff's toy bear

found only one familiar name—Paul Sondhoff. Walter became a house guest in Anny and Paul's apartment on that visit and on a later occasion when he returned to Vienna with Rachel, his British wife. Rachel Foster (1923–2010) wrote: "Paul was a delight to be with and good company. No one would have guessed what he had been through."

On the Fosters' last visit, shortly before Paul left for the U.S., Paul gave the bear, a "prized possession," to Rachel for the family that Walter and Rachel would have someday. Walter wrote, "So the bear became a member of our family, our children were taught to treat him with respect because he was very old and had had a very bad experience during the war. It was a difficult decision to let the bear go to the museum. We miss him."

Unfortunately, the text on the wall where the bear is displayed reads in full: "Between 1941 and 1945, Paul Sondhoff was hidden in a small cupboard by his piano teacher in Vienna—a space so cramped that he later developed deformities. One of his few possessions was this clockwork bear which he kept with him in his hiding place." This assertion about "deformities" is repeated in the exhibit catalog, where an entire page is devoted to a photograph of the bear.

There are several reasons to doubt that assertion. Paul was quite short, probably not more than 5 feet tall, but he was not noticeably deformed. He was 19 years old, not a child, when he went into hiding in 1942. The attic space was probably a small room, not a cupboard, and Paul was not continuously confined there. In addition, Paul's nickname "Bibi" suggests that he was unusually small as an adolescent before the war.

Paul's bear powerfully evokes the cruelty of the Holocaust—the image of a small child hiding in fear, clutching a beloved object. The

reality of Paul's story, however, is perhaps more powerful, and certainly tells us much more about Paul himself than the inaccurate story that was presented by the Museum. Once one appreciates Paul's actual situation during those years–a young man in hiding not knowing what had become of his mother and younger sister–it is more likely that the bear belonged to Agnes, and he kept it in the hope that he could return it to her someday. Only when he learned after the war that Agnes was gone, did he relinquish it to a good friend.

In any event, Paul's wartime experiences and losses seemed to do little harm to his irrepressible spirit. Liza Trahan recounts a visit that Paul ("Bibi") made to her in July1952 when she was studying at Cornell University. On a walk across campus, they noticed several animal traps set out by the Zoology department, and a frantic sparrow caught in one of the cages. Paul figured out how to open the trap. He freed the sparrow, then a squirrel, and mischievously set about disarming other empty traps. Later, when they found the traps re–set, Paul commented only, "They are too efficient for us." Liza wrote that she "could not tell if irony, bitterness or resignation tinged his voice."[20]

Julius Dutka and Fort Ontario Safe Haven

Brothers Max and Julius Dutka, married Mandl family first cous-ins—Hedwig Schlafrig and Klara Mandl. Each of the marriages produced two children born in Vienna. Neither of the marriages, however, ended well. By the time of Hitler's takeover of Austria, both couples were divorced. All but one member of the two families died in the Holocaust— Max, Hedwig, Klara, and their four offspring. The one survivor, Julius Dutka, had a remarkable journey.

Dutka siblings–Julius (standing left) Max (seated center), Alice, Ludwig, and Adolf Vienna, 1907

Like many Austrian Jews after the Anschluss, Julius fled to Italy, where he was interned at Ferramonti, a concentration camp south of Naples. Although not an extermination camp, Ferramonti was a place of internment for Jewish refugees. After the downfall of Mussolini, the Italian dictator and Hitler ally, in late 1943, the Ferramonti internees were freed. Many, however, including Julius, had nowhere to go as their homelands were still in Nazi hands.

In June, 1944, President Franklin Roosevelt, at the urging of Harold Ickes, Secretary of the Interior, agreed to a plan to house 1,000 European refugees at a former military base named Fort Ontario in Oswego, NY. Roosevelt circumvented the rigid immigration quotas by identifying these refugees as his "guests," but that status gave them no legal standing and required their return to Europe once conditions permitted. In Naples, Italy, more than 3,000 people applied to be one of Roosevelt's guests. Of these, 982 were chosen based on whether they were part of a family group, a community group, or a group that had worked together; greatest need; and a cross section of skills that would be needed to maintain the shelter. No families with healthy males of military age were accepted. Family groups were not to be separated. As many people as possible who had been in concentration camps were accepted.

It is not clear why Julius, a 58-year-old single person, was selected or what skills he offered. At 5 feet 3 inches tall, he weighed 85 pounds. In Vienna, he had been the editor of "Dutka's Maschineenmarkt," an ad–only newspaper for buying and selling machinery, although he had literary aspirations. While in Oswego, Julius copyrighted two plays, neither ever published. In his Declaration of Intention to apply for U.S. citizenship, Julius listed his occupation as "publisher."

Advocates for the Fort Ontario refugees lobbied Congress and the President to allow them to stay in America. In December 1945, President Harry Truman ordered that the refugees be permitted entry as immigrants into the United States. As described by Ruth Gruber, an assistant to Secretary Ickes who had accompanied the group from Naples, Italy: "To enter the United States legally, they had to leave it. On January 17, 1946, the first three busloads, carrying ninety-five refugees, left camp at six in the morning. They drove across western New York State to Buffalo, where the community invited them to a roast-beef lunch in Temple Beth El. Then the buses traveled to

Niagara Falls and crossed the Rainbow Bridge to the town of Niagara Falls, Ontario, Canada. There they were greeted by George Graves, the American consul, who gave each refugee the longed–for visa embellished with a red seal and a ribbon. They drove back across the Rainbow Bridge and at last entered America."[21]

Julius Dutka crossed the Rainbow Bridge into the U.S. with visa in hand on Feb. 4, 1946. Julius went to live in New York City, where he hoped to make a living as a writer. He died, however, of heart failure on September 15, 1947. We do not know if, or when, Julius learned that his former wife Klara Mandl and their two children, Sigmund and Alice, had been killed in Europe.

Remarkably, one other Mandl family relation was among the Fort Ontario refugees. Olga Popper Blumberg was the mother of Herta Blumberg Friedmann (later Freeman), who emigrated with her husband Herbert Friedmann in 1938 from Vienna to Perth, Australia. (See Chapter 11.) How Olga, in 1944 a 74-year-old widow from Vienna, came to be in Italy and one of the Fort Ontario chosen is unknown. From Fort Ontario, Olga re-entered the U.S. at Niagara Falls on February 5, 1946, and thereafter lived in the New York metropolitan area, not far from another daughter, Gertrude Blumberg Ziffer, until her death in 1959.

Notes

1 On March 20, 1941, Melitta Aschkenes (see Chapter 8) wrote to her uncle David Mandl, both having resettled in the U.S., "We are very happy that you were now able to send the affidavits for Fritz and Gustav as well . . . One really has no idea what is going on there." The Affidavit executed by Lawrence White, a New York attorney who described himself as a friend of David Mandl, was obviously to no avail.

2 Alan Rosen, *The Wonder of Their Voices: The 1946 Holocaust Interviews of David Boder* (2010).

3 One such book with accompanying commentary has been published. Cara de Silva, ed., *In Memory's Kitchen: A Legacy from the Women of Terezin* (1996).

4 Schlafrig Family Papers Accession Number: 2014.538.1, 2014.538.2; Recipe Book https://collections.ushmm.org/search/catalog/irn531144.

5 Ursula Prokop *On the Jewish Legacy in Viennese Architecture: The contribution of Jewish architects to building in Vienna 1868–1938.*

6 Helmut Weihsmann, *In Wien erbaut: Lexikon der Wiener Architekten des 20. Jahrhunderts* (2005).

7 Turi, Zsuzsa. Interview 51682. *Visual History Archive*, USC Shoah Foundation, 2001.

8 Helene's parents were Joseph (b. 1858) and Rosa Zaker (1864–1940) Goldberger from Oderberg in Schlesien (aka Wola Radiszowksa). Joseph's brothers Bernard and Sam emigrated to the U.S. in the 1880s. Sam settled in Baltimore, shortening his name to Goldberg. Bernard (1861–1950) settled in New York and was the father of Louis Joseph Goldberger (1890–1966). See Chapters 9 and 10. Joseph may have come to the U.S. with his brothers, but elected to return to Europe.

9 *Walter Kohn: Personal Stories and Anecdotes Told by Friends and Collaborators*, pp. 60–62, 173–76 (2003).

10 The Meldeauskunft (city registration) shows different addresses for Alfons and Helene, with the children, beginning in September, 1936.

11 Alfons Sondhoff, born Mar. 24, 1893 in Ostrau, was buried in Vienna's Zentralfriedhof IV on Sept. 5, 1940. His gravestone, probably erected after the war by Paul and Alfons' sister Anny Sonderling Ceiger, now includes a memorial to Helene and Agnes.

12 https://memorial–ebensee.at/website/index.php/de/geschichte/18–salzkammergut–1938–45/15–lager–traunsee; http://www.aufrichtigs.com/01–Holocaust/Walter_Aufrichtig_–_Traunkirchen–2.htm

13 Anny Sonderling, born in 1906 in Neu Oderberg, did not change her name to Sondhoff as her brother had done.

14 Frau Mattha's name and subject taught come from the memoir of Elizabeth Trahan, a first–hand observer of these events. Another source, who heard the story from Paul only after the war, recalled that it was a piano teacher.

15 Elizabeth Welt Trahan, *Walking with Ghosts: A Jewish Childhood in Wartime Vienna*, pp. 101, 140–145 (1998).

16 C. Gwyn Moser, *Jewish U–Boote in Austria*, 1938–1945, in Simon Wiesenthal Center Annual, Vol. 2, 1985; Brigitte Ungar–Klein, *Schattenexistenz: Jüdische U–Boote in Wien 1938–1945*.

17 Max Ceiger, 1896–1989, was the uncle of Elizabeth "Liza" or "Liesel" Welt Trahan, 1925–2009, who was in Vienna throughout the war and whose memoirs recount most of what is known about Paul and Anny during the war years. Liza Trahan and Paul remained friends after both came to live in the United States. Elizabeth Welt Trahan, *Ten Dollars in My Pocket: The American Education of a Holocaust Survivor*, pp. 180–183 (2006).

18 Also in attendance at Nellie's funeral was Julius Kahn, the New York attorney who assisted the family with emigrations from Europe in the 1930s. See Chapter 10. Letter from Hattie Kahn Kesselman to Eleanor Goldberger Friedman, Jan. 29, 1965.

19 Walter Foster, *All for the Best or The History of Young Walter*, privately printed 1993.

20 Elizabeth Welt Trahan, *Ten Dollars in My Pocket: The American Education of a Holocaust Survivor*, pp. 180–183 (2006). Suzanne Bardgett, Project Director of the Holocaust Exhibit at the Imperial War Museum, provided an exhibit catalog and facilitated contact with Walter and Rachel Foster. Sandra Nagel of the IWM assisted in locating Cristel Sondhoff and the Gaiser family in Laufen, Germany. Information also came from June Entman's personal interviews and correspondence with Cristel Gaiser Sondhoff, Monika and Tobias Gaiser, Walter and Rachel Foster, Herbert Neuhaus, Gertrude Ehrlich, and Elizabeth Welt Trahan.

21 Ruth Gruber, *Haven: The Dramatic Story of 1,000 World War II Refugees and How They Came to America*, p. 279 (1978); https://www.safehavenmuseum.com/.

Mandls Killed in the Holocaust

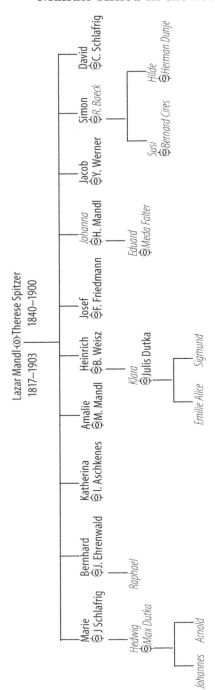

* Names in italics are those who died in the Holocaust

13.

LOST IN THE HOLOCAUST

HELENE GOLDBERGER SONDHOFF b. 1893 and ALMA AGNES SONDHOFF b. 1930, mother and daughter cousins of Louis J. Goldberger, were deported from Vienna in June 1942 and murdered shortly thereafter at Maly Trostinec, Belarus. (See Chapter 12.)

Memorial to Helene and Agnes on Alfons Sondhoff's gravestone in
Vienna Zentralfriedhof IV, Tor, Group 20a, Row 31, grave 51.

JOHANNA MANDL MANDL b. 1862 was the only one of the ten Mandl siblings (see Chapter 1) to die in the Holocaust. A widow since 1929, Johanna was deported from Uherske Ostroh, Czechoslovakia to Thereisenstadt on January 31, 1943, along with her son **EDUARD MANDL** b. 1894 and his wife **MALVINE "MEDA" FALTER MANDL** b. 1903. Eduard, a veteran of the Austrian army, and Meda were further transported to Auschwitz on February 1, 1943 where they were killed on March 8, 1943. Johanna died at Thereisenstadt on March 6, 1943.[1]

Herman, Siegmund, Eduard, Johanna Mandl, ca. 1910

Johanna, Eduard, Herman, Meda Mandl, Uherske Ostroh, ca. 1926

Johanna and Meda Mandl, ca. 1936

Rabbi Simon Mandl of Neutitschein, Czechoslovakia, and his youngest daughter Liesl died before the Holocaust. Simon's widow, **Rose Baeck Mandl** b.1871, was one of Rabbi Leo Baeck's four sisters who died in Thereisenstadt. She was deported there on July 4, 1942 and died on September 17, 1942. Simon and Rose's daughter, **Hilde** and her husband **Hermann Dunje** disappeared in the Holocaust. Someone named Hermann Dunje born in 1883 is listed as having been deported on October 24, 1941 from Berlin to the Lodz ghetto, and later to Chelmno, Poland where he was killed on May 4,1942, but there is no mention of Hilde Mandl Dunje in any of the Holocaust databases.

In 1941, Simon and Rose's daughter, **Suzi Mandl Cires** b. 1903 and her husband **Dr. Bernard Baruch Cires** b. 1901 moved from Berlin to Leipzig Germany where Bernhard had found employment at the Jewish Hospital. A distant cousin of Bernard's in the U.S., Esther Kaye, had executed an Affidavit of Support for the Cires to obtain a visa to the U.S., but it had expired before they were able to take advantage of it. In early 1941, both Susi and her uncle David Mandl, now living in the B'nai B'rith Home in New York, wrote to Esther asking for a new Affidavit. David wrote, in part:

You know, dear Miss Kaye, that this is a question of saving two young, capable people who are willing to do any kind of work, I myself, her old uncle cannot do anything to help them. Until Hitler came, I had been a manufacturer in Vienna, Austria for 44 years, and have to be very grateful for having been admitted to this home with my wife, as a former old member of the B'nai B'rith Lodge in Vienna. Let me implore you, dear Miss Kaye, to do this work of kindness very soon, it may save these young creatures from actual perishing.'

Uncertain of his English, and given the import of the matter, David sent his letter in German to his niece Melitta Aschkenes (see Chapter 8), who translated and sent it on to Esther Kaye Freeman, who replied on March 24, 1941 from her home in Connecticut:

My dear Mr. Mandl

Thank you for your letter. I am indeed glad to make the acquaintance of Suzi's uncle. After reading your letter I planned to go to Yonkers and speak with you personally, but unfortunately my plans did not materialize.

Naturally I am very sympathetic and anxious to help Suzi and Bernard. I was greatly impressed with them when I met them in Berlin in 1935—I think Suzi is a remarkable person and nothing would make happier than to help take her out of her misery. ...

. . .

I think Suzi and Bernard are being a little misled. When I made out their affidavit, I showed a financial bank statement of $6,000. Little did they know that the money was placed in my name by a group of people for a short time just in order to make my financial rating a good one. The moment their affidavit was mailed, the money was replaced in its proper channel.

During my teaching career I contributed toward a pension fund. Because of family responsibility since my father's death—1930—that represents my life's savings. In June my teaching career comes to an end because married women are not allowed to teach in Connecticut, and the money will be paid to me.

I am willing to turn this money over to a steamship company to pay for passage for Suzi and Bernard if I knew definitely that they would receive it. I am too poor a girl and have slaved too hard in my life for that money to have it fall in the hands of a swindler. The Hapag company does not stand investigation. One other company contacted me, and I had a lawyer from New York go to their office and they too were swindlers. If I am to turn over the only money I have in the world—naturally, I am anxious to have it do the job I want it to—and not butter the bread of fakirs.

...

I shall be glad for your advice. Please remember that I must do this alone—there is absolutely no one to help. ... My heart aches for Suzi and Bernard. They are such a high–class couple—just wonderful people and I do want to help them. Please advise me.

Very truly yours,

Esther K. Freeman

Bernard and Suzi Mandl Cires were killed at Auschwitz on July 13, 1942.

Simon and Rose Baeck Mandl family in Neutitschein, Czechoslovakia, ca. 1920

There are also no survivors among the children and grandchildren of Dr. Heinrich Mandl and his wife Bertha Weisz, both of whom had passed away by 1932. Their son **GEORG MANDL** b. 1902, died at Auschwitz on August 22, 1942. Their daughter **KLARA MANDL DUTKA** b. 1899 was divorced from Julius Dutka, who survived the war. (See Chapter 12.) Klara, her daughter **ALICE EMILIE DUTKA** b. 1924, and son **SIGMUND DUTKA** b. 1925 were all killed in the Holocaust.

HEDWIG SCHLAEFRIG DUTKA b. 1882, youngest child of Marie Mandl and Jonas Schlaefrig, was married to, and in 1935 divorced from, MAX DUTKA, brother of Julius. Their two children were JOHANNES DUTKA b. 1914 and ARNOLD RAFAEL DUTKA b. 1921. Max was killed at Maly Trostinec on August 21, 1942. Hedwig and her second husband SALOMON FRIED b. 1877, were deported on November 23, 1941 from Vienna to Kowno, Lithuania, where they were killed.

Johannes and Arnold Dutka fled to Belgium from Vienna shortly after the Anschluss in 1938, but were unable to escape further. A story told by one of their Dutka uncles is that one of the brothers left first, and after arriving in Belgium, called home to tell his brother to follow and be sure to bring his violin. Arnold was deported on September 20, 1943 from Belgium to Auschwitz where he was killed. Johannes is presumed to have been killed as well.

Hedwig, Johannes, Max Dutka ca. 1920

Arnold Dutka. Photo from Belgian immigration files of those deported by German SS to concentration camps between 1942–1944.

R to l: Hedwig Schlafrig Dutka with her sister–in–law Paula Bereiter Dutka,
sons Arnold & Johannes, and Paula's son Harry ca. 1932

Bernhard Mandl's son, **Raphael Mandl** born in 1898, was a civil servant living in Budapest when he was deported to a labor camp in 1943. (See Chapter 12.) He did not return.

Raphael Mandl ca. 1915

Sisters Judith Kohn Mandl and **THERESA KOHN REISZ** left Vienna with their husbands and children, arriving together in Belgium in September 1938. Thereafter, the families were separated. Judith, husband Siegmund, and children Otto and Edith were all in the U.S. by March 1940. (See Chapter 10.) Theresa's husband Jacob Reisz and daughter Gertrude arrived in the U.S. in 1948. Theresa, age 43, and her son **ALBERT REISZ**, age 21, were murdered in Auschwitz in 1944.

Judith Kohn Mandl and Theresa Kohn Reisz ca. 1918

Friederike Friedmann, wife of Josef Mandl, had two sisters—Sophie, married to Hugo Weiss, and Ernestine, married to Isidor Beinhacker. While Sophie and Hugo's sons emigrated to Australia after the Anschluss (see Chapter 11) , they could not convince their parents to leave Vienna. According to his grandson Ernest's memoir, Hugo Weiss believed that his service as an officer in the Austrian army would serve as a protection.

On January 26, 1942, **SOPHIE AND HUGO WEISS** and **ERNESTINE AND ISIDOR BEINHACKER** were deported from Vienna on Transport No. 15 arriving at Riga, Latvia on January 31. While the deportees were told that they were being relocated to the Riga ghetto, this was the same time as the Nazis were exterminating the Jews of that place. Transport No. 15 consisted of 1,200 Jewish deportees from Vienna; 508 people were older than 61, the average age on this transport was 56 years. Conditions were brutal: no food, water, facilities, or heat for six days confined in the railcars. Some died on the journey; many of the deportees did not make it to the ghetto. After their arrival, elderly and sick people as well as children were put on vehicles that waited for them at the station. Those vehicles were gas vans, in which all of them were murdered. Others were sent directly from the station to the Rumbula Forest, where they were murdered.[2] Because the Weiss's and Beinhackers were between ages 64 and 73, it is assumed they were murdered very shortly after arrival in Riga on 31 Jan 1942.

Sophie Friedmann Weiss ca. 1938

Hugo Weiss with grandson Ernest, ca. 1938, shortly
before Ernest and his parents left Vienna for Australia

Siegmund Werner, Henrietta Werner Mandl's first cousin featured in Chapter 3 was the eldest of Josef and Johanna Werner's four children. Although Siegmund died in 1928, his siblings lived long enough to become victims of the Holocaust.

Werner siblings, l to r: Siegmund, Ida, Julius, Ludwig ca. 1894

On August 27, 1942, **IDA WERNER SALZER,** age 72, her brother **LUDWIG WERNER,** age 69, and Ludwig's wife **HELENE SAFFIR WERNER,** age 66, were deported from Vienna to Thereisenstadt.[3] Ludwig died there on Sept. 30, Ida on October 8, and Helene at some later date. In June 1945, the following obituary announcement appeared in *Aufbau,* an international journal for German–speaking Jews published in New York.

Im Namen unserer Familie zeigen wir an, dass unser geliebter Onkel und Schwager

Dr. LUDWIG WERNER

ehem. Hofrat der Oesterr. Bundesbahnen, Wien.

und seine tapfere, treubesorgte Frau, unsere Schwester und Tante

HELENE WERNER

geb. Saffir

im Lager Theresienstadt im Jahre 1943 von ihren Qualen befreit wurden. Wer dieses seltene Paar gekannt hat, wird mit uns trauern.

Dr. Theodor Werner, London
Dr. Eric Werner, Cincinnati
Capt. Robert Werner, RAF.
Edith R. Werner, Haifa
Rose Schwarz-Werner, London
Stella J. Werner, Polen

Hans Saffir, Detroit
Dr. Fritz Saffir,
    Baildon, Yorkshire
Grete Lang,
    Lyon, France
Pvt. George Lang, Italy.

English translation: "On behalf of our family, we announce that our beloved uncle and brother–in–law Dr. Ludwig Werner, Former Hofrat der Oesterr, Federal Railways, Vienna, and his brave, faithful wife, our sister and aunt Helene Werner born Saffir were freed from their torments in the Theresienstadt camp in 1943. Anyone who knew this couple will mourn with us."

JULIUS WERNER b. 1869, professor and Greek scholar, and his wife HELENE DONATH WERNER, parents of the noted musicologist Eric Werner, were also killed by the Nazis.[4]

זצ״ל

May Their Memory Be A Blessing

Notes

1 Yad Vashem, Holocaust (Shoah) Deportation Database. Yad Vashem, The World Holocaust Remembrance Center in Jerusalem Israel maintains a digitized database of Holocaust (Shoah) victims with documents from various sources evidencing deportations, internments, and murders. Much of the specific data in this chapter comes from those sources.

2 Yad Vashem, Holocaust (Shoah) Deportation Database.

3 Yad Vashem, Holocaust (Shoah) Deportation Database

4 Fraenkel, Josef, Mathias *Acher's Fight for the "Crown of Zion,"* Jewish Social Studies 16, no. 2 (1954), p. 126 n. 30; http://www.jstor.org/stable/4465223.

About the Cover Portrait

Photograph. Hand written on reverse side:
"Lazar Mandl Gemeindebeamter im Szenice"

Painting

The painting of Lazar Mandl on this book's cover resides with Lazar's great-grandson, Tony Mandl of Sydney, Australia. We know nothing of the portrait's artist, its creation, or how it came to be in Australia, only that it appears to have been painted from one of the only two photographs we have of Lazar (1817-1903).

We do know from Paula Mandl Pentley's memoir, quoted in Chapter 7, that toward the end of his life, her grandfather Lazar lived in Mistelbach, Austria with his daughter and son-in-law, Marie and Dr. Jonas Schlafrig. This fact may be a clue to the portrait's creation.

Dr. Jonas Schläfrig, born in 1833 in Zolkiew in Galicia, received his doctorate in Lviv in 1857. From 1894 to 1910 he was a general practitioner physician and leader of the Jewish community in Mistelbach. As the story is told in a museum exhibition commemorating Mistelbach's Jewish community:

"One day, a patient came to Dr. Schläfrig in the practice at Hauptplatz 12. He was very ill, but had no money for examination or even for treatment. The doctor treated him [nevertheless] until he was healthy again. After a few weeks, the recovered patient came to the doctor, and brought him a painting as a 'thank you.' The patient, a painter by profession, had painted the doctor instead of paying. Dr. Schläfrig was very happy, but felt that in reality he looked a bit friendlier."

This painting was passed down to Jonas' granddaughter Helga Schläfrig; after she passed away in Vienna in June 2020, it was made available to the Mistelbach Memorial.

Not only is the style of the two portraits—Lazar's and Jonas'—similar, but Jonas' portrait looks as if it may have been painted from the photograph of Jonas with his daughter Hedwig that can be seen on the wall display to the left of the portrait. Perhaps, therefore, Dr. Schläfrig's grateful patient painted not only Jonas, but also his father-in-law Lazar Mandl, who was, in Paula's memory, "a wonderful old man with … beautiful dark kind eyes."

Historian Brigitte Kenscha-Mautner with portrait of Dr. Jonas Schläfrig
at the Mistelbach Jewish community memorial exhibition.

Name Index
(Numbers after name and dates indicate chapter(s))

Non-Family Members

As this book evinces, the author has a passion for family photographs; here are a couple more:

Entman famiy, l-r: Michael, June, Rachel, and Howard Entman. April 28, 2009

June Entman with Grandchildren, l-r: Alex, Jack, and Abby Hatch 2020

About the Author

June F. Entman, born in Brooklyn New York in 1945, grew up in Atlanta Georgia. She earned degrees from Smith College, the University of Chicago, and the University of Memphis School of Law. She is Emeritus Professor of Law at the University of Memphis and resides with her husband Howard Entman in St. Augustine, Florida.

Made in United States
Orlando, FL
26 October 2022

23880824R00104